Of Human Freedom

Books by Jacques Barzun

THE FRENCH RACE

RACE, A STUDY IN SUPERSTITION

OF HUMAN FREEDOM

DARWIN, MARX, WAGNER

CLASSIC, ROMANTIC, AND MODERN

TEACHER IN AMERICA

BERLIOZ AND THE ROMANTIC CENTURY

GOD'S COUNTRY AND MINE

MUSIC IN AMERICAN LIFE

THE ENERGIES OF ART

THE MODERN RESEARCHER

THE HOUSE OF INTELLECT

SCIENCE: THE GLORIOUS ENTERTAINMENT

Translations

BECQUE'S LA PARISIENNE

PLEASURES OF MUSIC

DIDEROT'S RAMEAU'S NEPHEW

MIRBEAU'S THE EPIDEMIC

MUSSET'S FANTASIO; A DOOR SHOULD BE OPEN OR SHUT

FLAUBERT'S DICTIONARY OF ACCEPTED IDEAS

NEW LETTERS OF BERLIOZ

BERLIOZ'S EVENINGS WITH THE ORCHESTRA

FOUR PLAYS BY COURTELINE

BEAUMARCHAIS'S FIGARO'S MARRIAGE

JACQUES BARZUN: OF HUMAN FREEDOM

REVISED EDITION

GREENWOOD PRESS, PUBLISHERS
WESTPORT, CONNECTICUT

Library of Congress Cataloging in Publication Data

Barzun, Jacques, 1907–
  Of human freedom.

    Reprint of the 1964 ed. published by Lippincott,
Philadelphia.
    Includes bibliographical references and index.
    1. Culture--Addresses, essays, lectures.
2. Democracy--Addresses, essays, lectures. I. Ti-
tle.
[CB151.B3 1976]   909   76-47651
ISBN 0-8371-9321-4

Copyright 1939, © *1964 by Jacques Barzun*

Originally published in 1964 by J. B. Lippincott Company,
Philadelphia

Reprinted with the permission of Dr. Jacques Barzun

Reprinted in 1976 by Greenwood Press, Inc.

Library of Congress Catalog Card Number   76-47651

ISBN 0-8371-9321-4

Printed in the United States of America

To Wendell Hertig Taylor

Preface to the Revised Edition

A HUNDRED years ago, when the public world, being more provincial seemed smaller, the habit grew up of calling the contemporary battle of ideas an "age of transition." There was reason to believe that the past had exhibited, and the future would again exhibit, a more settled order than the present. By overuse, such references to "our age of transition" became a platitude and a joke: every age was seen to be transitional, every age a theater of strife. Yet the sophisticated appreciation of the joke does not abolish the fact that the great struggles of mankind over systems of government and of beliefs do come to an end, whether through victory, compromise, fatigue, or something of each: after the Protestant Reformation, the monarchical state; after the French Revolution, the rule of the liberal bourgeoisie. Each decade or each year of the second phase may still be regarded as transitional, but the quality and the intensity of change differ in degree from their counterparts in the first phase, the wars of religion and those of the revolution and Napoleon. What matters then to the student of his own time is the speed, length, and finality of the "transitions" going on before his eyes.

As I reread the present book for its reissue after a quarter century, I was struck by how little the western world had moved away from the anxieties and contentions of twenty-five years ago. Some names and labels have changed, of course: we no longer say "fascist" in the same sense or quote Mussolini, nor are our statesmen and publicists generally the same men. But policies and philosophies have not changed, and the "great" events of the period have been

vii

inconclusive. Socialism is no more triumphant or actual than liberalism; and no more than in 1939 are we at peace or at war; we teeter on the brink of the Third as we did then of the Second; we are still embroiled in race conflicts, and with no better understanding of their intellectual origins; we have totalitarianism at our door and are still seeking some opposing system of democratic ideas; we lament the "materialism" in our lives and lack a tenable philosophy to replace it, while we ignore or misuse the pragmatic principle; we are still dissatisfied with our mass education and continue to suffer from its looseness, despite the disenchantment of intelligent opinion with the progressive school; indeed, we still endure the debilitating attitudes of that schooling, which is now at work in our institutional life through the applications of social science: the organization man and his doings, from tests to brainstorms, are but the child-centered school writ large. And the medium in which our discussions and stale discoveries are expressed is the language whose corruption by pedantry and pretentiousness (and not, as Orwell thought, by politics alone) was well advanced thirty years ago.

On two great subjects also treated in this book, Art and Science, we do appear to have moved forward, or at least left our old positions behind. Modernism in art has been accepted throughout the West, and with such a depth of respect, even by the inarticulate mass, that the sign of the avant-garde today is to abandon the very notion of Art in favor of some act or piece of reality which shall rebuke artistry and hold the too devout public at arm's length. As for Science, a renewed interest in its workings is kept lively by the spectacle of man in outer space and of the ballet performed by the growing troupe of atomic particles. None of these manifestations was present or imaginable in 1939, and consequently some portions of two of the chapters at hand must be read as historical testimony.

Yet it is not stretching the facts to say that in a searching view of the present even those portions are not out of date. On the one hand, the new entertainment provided by science, like the new educational concern and enlarged popular literature about it, have not materially changed the widespread confusion about its nature, limits, and proper role. And on the other hand, the artistic revolution by which Philistinism has been purged and Experiment enthroned as absolute has left unaltered—which is to say unresolved—two of the questions I raised in 1939: the place of art and artists in a democratic society and the relation of the works produced since 1920 to the great innovations that preceded, from 1905 to the close of the First World War.

This last preoccupation of mine, which I could state more generally as the desire to find a cultural definition of the twentieth century, was in truth the immediate cause of this book. Several visits to the Paris Exhibition of 1937 had left me pondering the doubts and dilemmas that it presented without meaning to. Artistically, it marked a sharp decline from the Decorative Arts show of 1925. Politically, it was the first attempt of the fascist, communist, and Nazi propaganda machines to make "culture" an instrument of aggressive diplomacy. Socially, the poor management of the Exhibition, its heavy industrial style and listless "world outlook," forced the visitor to think again about popular government, about the economic and racial pretexts for regimentation, and about the deterioration of art, thought, and language due to demagogy and scientism. It seemed as if the heroes and martyrs of liberty since 1776 had missed their aim: here were the tangible, ostentatious results of emancipating mass feelings; here was what the people wanted.

These reflections confirmed my belief that politics and culture form a whole; and this in turn suggested that the definition of our century which I was seeking must begin with a statement about individual freedom and its prospects. Taken as an absolute, freedom could lead anywhere—as the fascist-communist-liberal actuality of the Paris Fair demonstrated. Taken pragmatically, that is, under the control of historical experience and a strict judgment of results, the ideal of the free and creative man made demands which were obviously not being met by the verbalizers, Utopians, and police-statesmen gathered at the Fair. It was to sum up these queries and conclusions in a phrase that my essay was called *Of Human*

Preface to the Revised Edition

Freedom and was offered as a sketch for a study of democratic culture.

It is perhaps proper to add that I should not have thought of rereading—much less of revising—the book without the urging of my friend George Stevens, its present publisher and in that older day my indulgent editor at the *Saturday Review*. It is his faith in the continued relevance of my chapters that has led me to discover it for myself and to hope that others could turn it to their use. And it is in support of his generous estimate that I have removed or replaced a good many distracting topical references and added a few explanatory notes. Here and there I have also shortened a discussion or corrected an awkwardness. But I have left tone and opinion what they were, despite the temptation of an older man to interfere with the spontaneity and even the perceptions of the young. Tampering would in any case have been futile or needless— futile if the interval of time has blurred the picture I drew in 1937–39, needless if, as I believe, the outlines are still clear.

J. B.

August 1, 1964

Contents

And I will war, at least in words (and should
  My chance so happen—deeds), with all who war
With Thought;—and of Thought's foes by far most rude
  Tyrants and sycophants have been and are.
I know not who may conquer: if I could
  Have such a prescience, it should be no bar
To this my plain, sworn, downright detestation
  Of every despotism in every nation.

—BYRON

A State which dwarfs its men in order that they may be more docile instruments in its hands even for beneficial purposes will find that with small men no great thing can really be accomplished. . . .

—J. S. MILL

She had got to the bottom of this business of democratic government and found out that it was nothing more than government of any other kind. She might have known it by her own common sense, but now that experience had proved it, she was glad to quit the masquerade; to return to the true democracy of life, her paupers and her prisons, her schools and her hospitals.

—HENRY ADAMS

Royce, you're being photographed! Look out! I say *Damn the Absolute!*

—WILLIAM JAMES

Of Human Freedom

1   *Introduction: Culture and Tyranny*

WHEN our children ask us, twenty years from now, "What did you accomplish in those days?" we shall perhaps be glad to answer, like the French revolutionist after the Terror, "I survived." Those who look about them to-day are inclined to despair—to despair of accomplishment, of civilization, of life itself. Any five or ten years seem an eternity when they are years filled with hatred, poisoned faith, and unspeakable violence. Yet by an effort of the will over the impressionable senses it is possible to see in those same years—whether five or twenty-five— the emergence of a great lesson that we have fairly bought with the lives of others and the anguish of our own deepest selves.

Amid all the distractions of the contemporary chaos we have learned that the things worth living for, the things we lump together under the name of culture and civilization, have to be defended at first hand. Our old belief that by doing something else in the name of an ideal —usually something violent—we could at one stroke achieve an all-round felicity has once more proved an illusion. The events in Russia, Spain, China, Italy, Germany, India, Africa have made it perfectly clear that the absolute dogmas and authoritarian systems which bid for our admiration and support not only are not doing what is claimed for them but are doing just the opposite.

The governmental efficiency that kills, jails, or expels the men of science and art is not efficiency; the social revolution that makes life more uncertain, that turns moral independence into a capital crime and espionage into the chief of the liberal arts, is not social and not revolution. The scientific methods and philosophic creeds that make men less and less thinking creatures and more and more gullible automata are not scientific and philosophic, but pseudo-scientific and sophistical. They do not lead to ends, but to the forgetting of ends in the application of means. They narcotize the intelligent and mean death to the articulate.

In the United States as in every other democratic country, the need to-day is for a searching of the heart to discover what democracy really wants and how it can insure the fulfillment of its choice. It may choose death for itself and others; it may choose life on certain terms or unconditionally. Life without conditions can be achieved very simply by giving up and waiting—sitting and perishing in due course. Life under certain conditions of civilization means a fighting faith training its critical guns on what is daily offered us in the guise of government, education, science, art, dogma, cures, and creeds.

The necessity for this faith and this critical war in our own culture is the great lesson of the recent past. It is not so much a new discovery as the rediscovery of a forgotten truth. And with the rediscovery we have learned the reason of our forgetfulness: we had become weary and lazy; we wanted short cuts to happiness and peace; we hoped to find rules of thumb that would answer every purpose; we were willing to join a party, sign a pledge, even enlist in an army, provided it was guaranteed to bring about the end of our troubles, by which we really meant make the last claim on our intelligence. The "distrust of intelligence," the "retreat from reason," were names given in alarm to what was thought to be a movement and was after all only a desertion.

But if, as every symptom warns us, civilized life is the

strenuous goal of democracy, if a diversified and vigilant culture is at once the source and the product of successful democracy, then our duty is to go over the common assumptions about familiar things, scrape the rust off our habitual opinions and see if there is any bright metal beneath, or only an oxidized mass of crumbling prejudices.

The first of these prejudices is to believe that our choice is a political one when it is, as a matter of fact, cultural. We think that we can deal with matters that involve our life and liberty by acting as partisans, whereas the very thing we want can only be achieved by acting as artisans.[1]* I mean by this, taking and rejecting in the light of purpose, regardless of groups, labels, and the mock scrimmage of politics. I shall develop the point in my next chapter, but a single example now will make my meaning clear. People who appreciate the importance of education in a democracy often ask me whether I am for or against John Dewey and Progressive Education. The form of the question is political; it is a bid for a party vote, to which I return the cultural answer: I work *for* individualized teaching, *for* the breakdown of artificial divisions between school subjects, but *against* amateur phychiatry in the classroom and *against* the failure to teach the three R's. My interlocutor sometimes insists: "But are you for it as a whole, Yes or No? Don't sit on the fence!" As well ask, am I for the Atlantic Ocean? I swim in it with pleasure, but deplore tidal waves and fail to see a fence in the distinction.

The fence is of course as imaginary as the possibility of voting about the ocean. Education of any kind is not a whole. It is a name for a series of practices, some of which are absurd and some admirable. Why anyone should relinquish his sacred right of criticism and blind his judgment of concrete particulars by either endorsing or rejecting the abstract "whole" would be inexplicable, were it not for the presence of the political-minded among

* Superior figures refer to Notes at end of text.

us who see fences everywhere, too often across the path of those who are attending to their cultural business by re-ënforcing what they approve and combating what they deplore.

No doubt there are emergencies when we cannot take time to distinguish: we must leave a ship not wholly rotten and take to a dinghy not wholly sound, but creating false emergencies of this kind within a going culture is a form of sabotage which leads straight to the evils we would avoid. The all-or-none policy *is* the retreat from reason. It is the dueler's false heroism which risks two lives on a Yes or No. And the habit of giving and taking the challenge, which masquerades as Choice, prepares our minds for tyranny—tyranny being nothing but the forcing and accepting of a single answer to a diversity of problems. It is a blind, deaf, and dumb machine that repeats the same operation in all circumstances and regardless of what material is thrown to it.

The human mind at its best works in precisely the opposite way: in art, in science, in a truly progressive education or democratic society, it seeks to distinguish differences and to deal with each appropriately. Freedom is in this sense native to the human mind; but being difficult to establish in a world full of conflicting minds, it generates the institutions of political democracy. Democracy is thus the result and not the cause of our deep-seated desire for diversity, freedom, and tolerance. It follows—and this is the twofold thesis of this book—that culture must be free if men's bodies are to be free; and culture perishes if we think and act like absolutists. Tyranny, like its opposite, Charity, begins at home, but unlike it, alas, does not stay there. Before I go on to elaborate this point of view and warn of dangers by studying certain elements of present-day American culture a word or two must be said about the term "culture" as it should be understood in this book.

Introduction: Culture and Tyranny

For some people culture has acquired a bad name owing to its association with advertisements of five-foot shelves and quick methods for addressing the waiter in French. For others, who read sociology and anthropology, culture has come to mean all the ways of thinking and behaving in a given society. Between these two extremes there is a meaning which it is important to rescue from oblivion. In this sense culture means consciousness as opposed to brute fact, the pictures in our minds as opposed to measurable economic, political, or physical reality. This use of the word "culture" bestows no honorific title: the newspaper is culture as well as the obscurest poem; jazz is culture as well as the symphony. Culture naturally has roots in hard, unyielding, measurable things, but these do not infallibly determine it. Consequently freedom is possible and diversity inevitable. The material fact that transatlantic jet service is now commonplace may make us think of Europe as nearer or of ourselves as better than our ancestors, of scientists as demigods or of the capitalist system as justified by its fruits. The basic fact begins to take effect only when we have made some such inference from it, or, more often, when we have wrapped up the fact and the inference in a single image which is our "opinion" on the subject, so that if a discussion of science or progress or capitalism comes up, we say, "Take, for example, the fact that yesterday at this time I was in," etc. . . .

Opinion, we all instinctively feel, is vastly important for freedom. Nothing brings tyranny home to us so vividly as the stifling of opinion, and all the great political prisoners of history, from the Prisoner of Chillon down, have always boasted that their bodies might be in chains but their minds were free. That fact marks the superiority of a dungeon in the past over "liberty" in a modern totalitarian state. The new millennium promises the better life, but it turns ordinary men into suspicious, terrified, and cruel beasts, in whom the possibility of political democracy has died, because the cultural source of freedom has been quenched. In other words, the great fields of opinion in a culture are also fields of practice, for it is our beliefs that make us act as we do; it is through our acts that our opinions make a difference.

For us to-day, as I contend, the great difference running through all our activities and all our thoughts is that between absolutism and relativism; between uniformity and many-sidedness; between the rigid and the appropriate. To establish the thesis that men's bodies cannot long be free if their culture is shot through with absolutism, I shall try to unmask and to discredit on grounds of theory and practical reason the main forms of cultural absolutism. I shall begin by developing the point just made that Democracy is simply an age-old desire for a free culture; then go on to discover whether democratic culture is indeed decadent; analyze the effects of hostile tyrannies upon the modern artistic forms of that culture; and suggest an answer to the problem, What can a democracy expect from its people in the way of great social-minded art? I must next consider the way our minds and our desires create not only culture with a capital C but what we call reality with a capital R, and show how we can handle and change that reality without giving ourselves up to the irrational, to activism and violence.

Such a discussion necessarily leads us to examine the function of science, which is supposed to discover reality, and of social science, which is supposed to help improve it. On the borderline between the two grows superstition, to which attention must be paid in the form of race belief and the supposed "tyranny of words" which breeds propaganda. Opposing truth to propaganda, and persuasion to coercion, raises the question of education in all its forms: how to transmit a democratic culture unimpaired to the young without torturing or crippling them in the

8

process. Lastly, if abandoning violent creeds we rely on education as a means of improving the future, we must recognize the limitations of that improvement while refining on the directions it can take. This itinerary, if rightly drawn, should bring us back to the faith that democracy is a way of living and thinking which is prerequisite to all the other freedoms we want to attain.

But these landmarks along our journey are not the landscape itself. The journey through it will, I think, be found less abstract, richer in particulars. For the ideas and conduct of men engaged in the four great divisions of our cultural life—art, science, education, and government—will have to be shown in either their democratic or their absolutist guise. The teacher, the critic, the scientist and social scientist, the artist and the patron of the arts, the psychoanalyst, and the "statist" (as Bacon's contemporaries neatly termed the thinking politician) will be considered as they foster or mar the sum total of democratic life we enjoy. Our dealings with them will be critical and historical in method, but always contemporary in purpose. We accordingly turn the page and begin our consideration of democracy as a culture.

2   Democracy: A Culture

"DEMOCRACY is dying; Freedom lies murdered—in Central Europe, Russia, Cuba, China, and many other lands. After three hundred years of seeming success the historical evolution of modern peoples towards liberty is facing its Waterloo." We hear this plaint from all sides; we repeat it; we believe it. We must believe it because only thus can we understand the wholesale infliction of torture and death upon masses of men indiscriminately lumped together by race, class, religion, or politics. Inoffensiveness, age, intellectual eminence—nothing stays the hand of the executioner, for the Reason of State does not listen to reason, and the victims perish less because they are dangerous than because the new gods thirst for sacrifices.

In the wake of this factual demonstration follows the argument from fear. We are urged to give up democracy before it sinks and to adopt some system of force which will provide the two needful things of a new Feudal Age —food and protection. Democracy, so runs the tempter's voice, is a failure. It is feeble, inefficient, corrupt. It "levels down to mediocrity" and, by turning everyone's mind to sham politics, it enables the unscrupulous to fill their pockets.[1] What we need is a highly organized group system which will serve the tribe by enforcing a fair distribution of goods to all within it, and by dealing out exile or death to all without. Consequently, it is "Down with elections and parliaments, down with international ideas and

Democracy: A Culture

religions, down with differences of opinion and their utterance. Life on the planet is a bloody struggle in which
survival goes to the fiercest beast of prey. Man is a wolf to
man and wolves must hunt in packs. All else is theory,
moonshine, and speedy death."

Strangest of all, this argument against democracy has
been adopted by the communist opponents of fascism.
The Marxists tell us that democracy is a middle-class
ideal: middle class, therefore capitalist; capitalist, therefore doomed. Yet these same prophets of doom agitate for
the democratic defense of political prisoners and would
have us fight war and fascism at home; would have us go
to war abroad to fight fascism there, and at the same time
convincingly prove to us that fascism is born of war, or
else that it is a phase of capitalism, like democracy; or yet
again that it is the work of power-mad megalomaniacs—
the Hitlers and the Stalins.

This juxtaposition of ideas is enough to show that the
madness, if any, has been contagious, and that at least
half the contemporary chaos springs from the inside of
our heads, from our inconsistent notions, our panicky
generalities, our utter lack of historical sense,[2] our amaz-
ing belief that dictatorships, violation of treaties, shame-
less diplomacy, civil war, and wholesale massacre of
innocents are new, unheard-of things invented a short
while ago expressly to plague us.

It would be unkind to insist, for the feeling is strong
that somehow we have failed, and this sense of failure
must be an occasion less of chiding than of inward self-
reform. In a mood of productive humility we must all
acknowledge that we have failed first of all to control our
beliefs. We have believed in absolute democracy, absolute
personal freedom, absolute peace and fairness in international affairs. Liberals have imagined a slice of European
history characterized by absolute moral improvement; or,
on turning Marxist, by absolute middle-class evolution

11

grounded in material causes. And when these beliefs proved untenable they were replaced by the bugbear of absolute one-man rule and absolute chaos.

In the United States, the most obvious sign of these abstract absolutes is the general assumption that the single word "democracy" means popular government and personal freedom, combined with weak, inefficient, and corrupt rule; as if all these were inseparable, whence it is inferred that if you remove personal freedom you gain strength, and if you abolish personal liberties you are left with an incorruptible and efficient one-man despotism. This is a fatal series of confusions. What could be more popular, in the worst sense, than the present governments we call totalitarian? Did not their leaders rise to power by demagogy, and do they not maintain themselves by ceaseless bidding for popular support? Do they not serve Demos when they make a fetish of eliminating privilege, including the privilege of dissent, and when they exalt the virtues of the people, as if the masses had a monopoly of virtue and common sense? A great show of social equality and economic sharing, of racial brotherhood and national unity, is the truly popular reward of totalitarianism; while a uniform propaganda working hand in hand with censorship satisfies the mob passion for finding sovereignty and truth within itself. To reject critical intelligence as a weakness and to make blind Will triumph through weight of numbers is the paradise of the mass-minded. It is indeed one way of understanding democracy.

The fathers of the American Constitution knew all this when they spoke with hatred and contempt of the mob. Unfortunately, the demagogue-lover in every one of us has always interpreted these remarks as aristocratic disdain of the lower orders. We have thereby forgotten a valuable lesson, the lesson that any irresponsible gang is a mob, no matter what its class, its slogans, or its aims.

Democracy: A Culture

Democracy, absolute and thorough, is the barbaric ideal
of majority tyranny, the mass choosing a leader whom it
follows or dethrones according to the whim of the moment or the luck of events in war and peace: dictators are
saying no more than the truth when they boast that theirs
is actually a popular government.[3] But obviously this sort
of populism gives no guarantee of honest or efficient rule.
Like other governments, it may or may not be corrupt,
while it is invariably wasteful of the lives and energies of
men.

Freedom, or Free Democracy, is something very different and much more difficult to achieve. It is a balance between popular will and individual rights. It is a civilized
society that tries to establish diversity in unity through
the guarantee of civil liberties. It wants stability and
peace, but recognizing the dynamic character of society
it finds it must safeguard criticism as sacred and insure
the free expression of thought as an intellectual privilege
granted equally to all. This Rule of Equality is often mis-
understood, as will appear in a moment, but it states what
most Americans mean by democracy—namely that Everyman, as such, is entitled to protection against individual
or mob tyranny. The whole community may be against
him and yet he lives. In following common usage and
calling this more complicated scheme of life democracy
for short, the notion of an absolute democracy claiming
complete freedom for the majority (or for its leaders) must
be uprooted from our minds, cast out as a dangerous play
on the word "democracy."

The fog of ambiguity around this word also obscures
the important fact that in the so-called democratic countries, free democracy is constantly breaking down. From
the Dreyfus Affair in France to the vindication by the
Supreme Court of the most obscure victim of injustice,
we must always be fighting for causes that involve our
liberties. What we fight is an individual or group tyrant

exercising local oppression. "Subversives" blacklisted, books and plays banned in Boston, the Evolution trial in Dayton, and the application of gag rule or gun rule anywhere, are signs of the tyrannical spirit of man and which has nothing to do with particular creeds. To imagine the love of tyranny as the peculiar mental trait of certain peoples, or as the result of "madmen's" powers of persuasion, is absurd. Tolerance is the fruit of circumstance grafted upon desire: the bishop who would persecute his fellow Christian upon the placing of a comma in the articles of faith will become a mild and broad-minded man when alone among the Ubangis whom he is hoping to clothe and convert. Respect for human freedom depends variously on intelligence, habit, sense of impunity, or fear; it does not depend in any fated way on class, race, or nationality. On the one hand, democracy as commonly understood endlessly breeds and combats internal oppression; while in oppressed countries every shift in home policy, every appeal to popular prejudice and all the efforts of propaganda show that Demos cannot be ruled by force alone.

What, then, is the difference? If democracy is not an institution or a set of institutions, what is it? It is an atmosphere and an attitude; in a word—a culture. It is not infallibly lodged in particular countries, but is wherever we find it. In our democracy we constantly complain of our institutions, and quite rightly. We deplore the people's seemingly infallible gift for voting Incompetence into office; we despair of the corruption that nullifies equality. But we remain democratic because our freedoms, however circumscribed, enable us to fight for more. We do not want Russian trials, Paris riots,* or racial pogroms. The vote, the jury system, the right to print, symbolize as well as carry out our preference. Even when they

* Not only those of the last twenty-five years, but the long series dating back to the post–1870 fascism of Boulanger, Déroulède, and Maurras.

fail to work, they concentrate our desire for tolerance and make vivid to ourselves and our opponents the limits within which we want free play for our thoughts and acts.

Democracy is a culture—that is, the deliberate cultivation of an intellectual passion in people with intellects and feelings. Like most passions it is at times vague, heedless, even unpractical, but always as real as the affinity of dog and bone. This passion is older than we think. It is true that it has been rapidly spreading through the Western world for the last three hundred years, but as a desire and a goal, it is as old as Socrates and Jesus. As a political movement it has been reënforced by science, the French Revolution, and Romanticism; and if capitalism has also fostered it, it is because these movements occurred in a capitalist era. The connection is real but is far from being cause and effect. There were democrats under Feudalism, just as there were democrats in Greece, and there will always be such so long as there are men to think and therefore to think diversely. Many men, many minds, is the basis of democracy.

The comforting worth of this historical fact is that democracy has already withstood mighty onslaughts of fascism, and that it will take a lot of killing before it disappears from the face of the earth. It will outlive dictators, conspiracies, and loud-speaker mythologies because it is stronger than material interests, more selfish than common selfishness, and more independent of favoring conditions than the hardiest desert cactus. If anyone doubts that freedom survives in unlikely habitats, let him compare eighteenth-century England under a corrupt Parliament and a stubborn king with our own country in our own times. There are places in this great republic where men like Benjamin Franklin and Thomas Jefferson, or even moderates like David Hume and Dr. Johnson, could not to this day draw a free breath.[4] What bulwark would they—would anyone—have against the

Of Human Freedom

"democratic" tyranny of their neighbors? Sheriff and citizens, in a fit of intellectual vigor, would feel irresistibly impelled to save their local culture by forcibly expelling the dissenters. And even if Dr. Johnson's conservatism served to excuse his free speaking, what would be the fate of his three fellows—radicals and freethinkers as out of place as Jonah in the whale? And as for the harmonizing of their four voices, it is obviously beyond the skill of a community where democracy means no more than a zeal for gregarious uniformity. A larger society, with titled lords and bishops, with royal pomp and country squires, is not on those accounts necessarily less democratic than a villageful of despotic pygmies.

If we know where free democracy resides and what it consists in, and if we want to preserve it, we must naturally defend our Bill of Rights and Constitution and fight war and fascism. But fully as important is our obligation to let a democratic breeze into the chambers of our own house and our own brain, for it is there that democracy begins and also there that it begins to decay.[5] It is not enough to protest against flagrant public violations. Democracy, to maintain itself, must repeatedly conquer every cell and corner of the nation. How many of our public institutions and private businesses, our schools, hospitals, and domestic hearths, are in reality little fascist states where freedom of speech is more rigidly excluded than vermin because felt to be more dangerous? It is a constant fight to besiege these live fortresses. Death and martyrdom abroad become vivid irrelevancies compared to the guerilla fought from day to day under threat of dislike and dismissal by those in whom democracy is a practical and particular passion, and not merely an opportunity for frothy partisanship.

This precariousness of democracy, far from damping our spirits, should console us about the present. That democracy is a culture means that we individually possess

16

the power to uphold it; means that we cannot win or lose it all at once. The madness is in us and not in the dictator, if we think his violation of free democracy is an argument against it. Since when does a wave of burglaries reduce "Thou shalt not steal" to absurdity? Liberty, one and immutable, is impossible to achieve, but particular liberties are the reward of effort in a democratic culture. Only a sentimentalist or a cynic—there is in fact no difference between them—will despair because the dinner which restores his spent energy does not remove the need of future dinners. So long as we continue our efforts, within the bounds of social peace, we are practical and have a chance of success. So soon as we give up and in despair adopt violence, we deserve what we get. As the hard-headed Hobbes says, "Every man ought to endeavor Peace in so far as he has hope of obtaining it." And he might have added: more often than we think, the endeavor justifies the hope.

2

A certain sort of practical mind may object that in any country, democratic or not, it is economic power that determines privilege, and that so long as we have one law for the rich and one for the poor, all boasts of nation-wide freedom will be idle. This is a fact, but we must not let it hypnotize us. The economic question is as old as man, though its overt recognition is new. Who offers to solve it out of hand? No one; though many propose a wonderful series of intermediate steps. What then is the choice before us? It is this: Can the solution of the economic problem be more readily attained under our limping system of theoretical-practical liberties, or under a system of absolute-paternal dictation? That and nothing else is the issue.

If any person or group held the answer, it might conceivably be practical to give up the right to criticize and let them dictate. But it turns out, the world over, that general disbelief in the dictator's scheme is enough to halt or wreck his plan. Inertia is fatal and coercion achieves nothing but . . . coercion. Consequently, that system is the more practical which leaves as many thinking minds as possible to grapple freely with the realities that hamper us.

This relation of the general intelligence to reality is the key relation in the modern world. The old governing classes could deal with economic facts far more readily than we. They could listen to the great landowners or the weavers of wool and placate them in turn, the rest being temporarily left to starve. But the increasing size of nations and interdependence of industries confront us with a tangle of interests no simple formula can solve. One thing only is clear and that is the impossibility of a strict class government. Whether in fascist, communist, or democratic countries, the latest step in tacit political theory is the recognition that tolerating poverty is no longer safe. It is so unpleasant a reality that we hasten to clothe it with dignified names like Purchasing Power, Consumers' Strike, and Flow of Goods. But the reality beneath establishes against all reaction or sophistry the doctrine of social equality. All societies today are or seek the means of becoming egalitarian.

A great deal has been written on both sides about the popular slogan of Equality. On the one hand the signers of the Declaration of Independence have been called fools for putting their names to the "palpably false" statement that all men are born and created equal; and on the other, the expounders of Inequality have been attacked as schemers for snobbish privilege. The two parties have been struggling with each other rather than with the difficulty.

The source of the error lies in mistaking equality for similarity. Men, so runs the argument, are not equal, for look! some are clever and strong, others weak and stupid; some are scientists and some are street sweepers. The doctrine of equality has in fact nothing to do with personal character or acquired talent. It only asserts two things: one, that all men are to be treated alike in a few respects enumerated by law; the other, that the relative worth of any two men in the state being incommensurable, it is simplest and wisest to assume their equality. When a number of parts are indispensable to a machine, it is childish to argue which is more or less indispensable—the flywheel or the cotter pin. The analogy breaks down when the cost of replacing the smaller part is measured, but it is retrieved again in society by the fact that small parts form large classes who threaten ruin to the whole machine if left uncared for.

As a moving part, every social class is indispensable, at least until replaced. We still inflict or tolerate neglect of whole classes, trades, or geographical areas, but that neglect marks a limit in our powers, not in our insight. The welfare state means nothing else. It may be a complete or a mitigated failure in practice—that is a matter for debate; but it will go down in history as the first large-scale popularization of the idea that a substantial and permanent equivalence of comfort, health, and economic security is the only means of saving such civilization as we have. The argument is familiar: it is for my children's sake that children in the slums must be kept in health. This must now be extended to read: it is for my security of life and livelihood that the slums themselves must go.

The steps by which substantial equality of income, of medical service, of educational opportunity, and the resulting freedom from animal cares, are to be achieved involve a multitude of technical matters most of the world as yet knows little about. Thinking about them yields— I speak for myself—a profound consciousness of ignorance. But the political idea of *assuming* equality from the outset relieves us of the questions which in present society form the greatest single obstacle to a better life. It is this same assumption of equality which in ordinary intercourse makes life not only pleasant but possible. If friends at my table were to be rationed according to their intelligence or moral worth, we should come to blows and never eat.

In the family, provided it is democratically run, everyone receives equivalent treatment: food and clothing appropriate to age and condition; training according to ability and inclination. At that point the means generally give out and social inequality or iniquity—it is the same thing —begins. Inequality limits everyone, including the rich, in freedom of movement, choice of friends, and pursuit of vocations; while it mars and shortens the lives of millions for whom the word "choice" has no meaning.

All this is appallingly true and the way out is by no means as plainly marked or as mysteriously preordained by History as some seem to think. The great danger is that seeing two needful things, a world physically fit to live in and a culture favorable to the free play of mind, we will strive in passionate spurts after intermediate goals that shut out one or the other of our desires. To relieve hunger we will jettison the first fruits of democratic freedom by regimenting everybody and his soul; while as upholders of culture and civilization we will shrink from losing our liberties in the doubtful hope of feeding anonymous millions. Those who face the dilemma as a dilemma are nowadays branded with the odious name of Liberal, whereas those who impale themselves on one of the horns offer up thanks that God made them men of action.*

Paradoxically enough, action, force, violence, are at-

* The comparison, which has often been made, of the Liberal to Hamlet is a misreading of the play. Hamlet "acts" almost from the beginning, and, far from hugging indolence, sets off a revolution and ends by strewing the stage with corpses.

tractive shorts cuts to the weary. History can show page upon page of interregnums when for fifteen or twenty years everybody was active, forceful, "practical." Those are the periods of civil war, the "times of troubles." In the end, the real efficiency turns out to be hard brain-work by a king or minister who begins the task of reconstruction by assuming the equality of groups and interests and persons within the state.

In our day the boasts of efficiency, brisk action, elimi-nation and extermination, purging and purifying, are so many admissions of *in*efficiency and panic fear. To say "off with his head" is not to govern but to shirk governing.

The answer to difficulty never lies in theatricalism. The dilemma cannot be solved by anything but intel-ligent action, which means not intelligence or action by itself, but both working together at the multitude of particular problems that constitute the total difficulty. In a democracy, of all places, we must not pretend that "intelligent" is a term of praise and despise it in our hearts. If the economic realities I spoke of before are increasingly hard to get at, the political problems with which they are entangled are even more complex, and no machinery other than the human brain can cope with them. It matters little whose brains it is, provided we do not all abdicate responsibility in our neighbor's favor. Shortly before Austria went fascist, in 1938, Schuschnigg is reported to have said that 25 per cent of the population were for him, 25 per cent for Hitler, and that the rest would go the way the cat jumped. This principle deserves the name of Schuschnigg's Con-stant. The only doubt is whether he did not grossly ex-aggerate the number of those having opinions.

Except in moments of national stress,—war, elections, party rallies, or Olympic Games,—how real is the com-munion of ideas or feelings among the parts of a nation?

In other words, how fluid and free is our culture, upon which depends not only the particular choice of the moment but the possibility of making future choices? We are compelled to admit that for many the only social question is to keep alive. *Primum vivere, deinde philosophari;* first have a job, then perhaps have opinions. It is a small articulate minority who, having opinions, assume that their preoccupations are high matters; their knowledge and desires common knowledge and common desires.[6] Yet so strongly do they project their feelings that they succeed in indoctrinating large masses of men with at least the catchwords of the contest, and use the masses' perennial wants as motive power for their side.

This mixture of realism and deception in political struggles is what makes government a cultural problem. When we alternately use and deplore superstition, spread or combat propaganda, we are not shadowboxing but coping in earnest with opinion; the whole aim of disinterested leadership and education being to raise the quality of common opinions and make them fit the increasing complexities in our path. At any moment in the life of a democracy, there are real predicaments and verbal formulations. The verbalizing is made up of vague feelings, new ideas, old tags of doctrine and hints of future bliss. Politics is the attempt to hitch them all together and pull out of the morass in some one direction.

It is here that the rival methods of free democracy and fascism most clearly show their difference. Free democracy permits everyone to take part in life as a cultural agent, and not merely as a pawn. It secures him the privilege of forming and criticizing opinions. This is not an idealization of the facts: the democratic tendency is to publish, argue, circulate novelty, defend small sects and vindicate original minds.* Totalitarianism of every

---

* A citizen of the United States or the United Kingdom, for example, can buy the works of Veblen or Marx or Burke or Saint Augustine;

brand, though unable to escape the necessity of palaver,* tends to stay at the lowest level of conceptual effort by telling the masses they are the bearers of light or the intended victims of foreign plotters, imperialists, warmongers. And behind the barrage of words, the complicated tasks of government go on as usual in the hands of the few.†

The cultural basis of democracy is, I hope, proved: Government is a medium as well as a device and we breathe in it twenty-four hours a day.

3

It now remains to see what kind of intelligence, what individual faiths and habits of mind, make for democratic culture. A century and a quarter ago, Tocqueville visited the United States and said, "I know of no country in which there is so little independence of mind and freedom of discussion as in America." His whole report on the young republic, which he had approached with sympathy and enthusiasm, is pervaded by this limitation, so that the motto of his book could have been "Democracy in America is not Free Democracy."

Things have changed since 1831. The United States *is* a free democracy, but we who live in it are still afraid of discussion. We prefer kindness to intelligence, boosting to knocking, conformity to criticism. We dread unpopularity and so court one another with lies, as minions used to court princes, to their joint peril in this world and the next. From our habit of combining in groups to extort blackmail from some other temporarily helpless group (which retaliates at the first opportunity), we have

can talk as he pleases about politics, consort with whom he chooses, and vote without supervision from the soldiery. Instances of coercion exist, but they are still regarded as abnormal, shameful, and injurious.

* See Chapter 9.
† See Chapter 11.

come to forget the reason for our combining. Parties extort loyalty within, that they may extort material advantage without: seemingly a "practical" move but one
which, systematically carried out, kills freedom—specifi-
cally, free talk, free action, free friendship, free fancy.[7]

The trouble is that we undervalue the comforts of conscience and the power of ideas, while grossly overvaluing
our brute strength in a world choked with groups,
leagues, guilds, and unions. Oddly enough, we concede
the power of ideas in our opponents. We call their ideas
"myths" and treat them with a kind of awe, not seeing
that our own faith in diversity, our own interest in ideas,
is a perfectly good and workable myth. By ideas I do not
mean pedantry or meditation. I mean simply attending
with all our mind to the matter in hand and resisting
the seduction of such absolutes as I shall define in a
moment. As for the man of ideas, he is anyone who uses
his head to cope with the difficulty before him; the il-
literate immigrant is as often a man of ideas as the college graduate is a dolt. The power to propel a thought
even a half inch beyond the vulgar notion is in fact the
only thing that divides the intellectual class from the rest.
The rest are no doubt the backbone of the nation, but as
in the human body so in the body politic, the backbone
stops just short of the head.

Holding radical opinions is by no means a guarantee
that one belongs to the thinking part. It is just as easy to
be blind on the Left as on the Right. The only difference
to human history is that the point of resistance to reality
comes sooner or later in chronological time. How to stick
to principle or social aim while facing facts as they are
is the peculiar problem for human intelligence in a
democratic culture, and this reliance on brain power
always implies that it is free, that the choice is real. Hence
the need of resisting absolutes—that is, party labels,
rigid loyalties, simple rules of thumb, easy or cynical

fatalism. Anybody can take sides when things are labeled "revolutionary," "reactionary," or "democratic." But what is it we are asked to believe, to consent to, to support? What value is there in opinions that flow from us like the saliva in Pavlov's dogs, at the ringing of a bell? And again, if our fate is mechanically ground out by the omnipotence of interests, then why indulge in so much talk and print? If talk and print play their part, then why handle them like a mace, incapable of flexible and pointed use?

The totalitarian may have said in his heart, "There is no justice," but the facts rebuke him. Has the democratic, popular opposition to the police state crystallized around material interests? Not in the least. It has become significant in defense of men representing Opinion in the arts and sciences: university professors, shy scholars, childlike mathematicians—all manner of mild life which is commonly thought to deserve pity and contempt. Basque children, poverty-stricken Jews, ignorant peasants, even remote tribes from the bush of unfamiliar continents—these have concentrated democratic passion, expressed in money and lives. Where is the interest? What miracle has united one-time antagonists, divided by politics and religion, if not a vast vested interest of Intellect against a totalitarian mass confessing that it has given up its will, its intelligence, and consequently its fate, into the hands of absolutists?

In the United States, where democratic culture is even now making lively efforts to insure its survival, by criticism, persuasion, and professions of faith, it would be insidious to separate by class, or in any other *a priori* fashion, the culture-carriers from the culture-destroyers. Each man does that for himself by taking his place. But the ideas that are in the air, the practices we find in use, can and must be tested for their fitness to serve democracy. I have tried to show in this chapter that free democ-

25

racy is a form of culture, a habit of thought that must be defended in the teeth of all oppressive forces, those within us as well as those around us. Those within us take the form of ideas; those around us we experience as legal or social coercion. To deal with the latter we must not underrate the power of the former. Seemingly indifferent in themselves, ideas can lead to freedom or slavery by controlling the minds of those who control the legal or social force.

I have shown in a previous work* by what steps the most remote and seemingly harmless scientific research has led to superstitious race-baiting in modern Europe. The academic idea has become an epidemic fact. It is first a cultural, then a political catastrophe. And we have only to look about us to find that the crassest and most destructive schemes invariably start by drafting art, science, and education on their side. Then the proscriptions begin. The same ideas can be windows on the world or strait jackets; they can paralyze or heighten our joys, resolve or arouse our fears. And with any idea, as I cannot repeat too often, it is our basic notion of its absolute truth and universal applicability that is our undoing. If we believe in absolute truths, how can we help murdering one another as heretics? And if that is indeed the practical way of using ideas to achieve peace and civilization, how can we help being saddled at a moment's notice with an absolute government which, quite possibly, will have got hold of some other absolute than our own?

We thoughtlessly repeat that the desire for absolutes is only the human desire for certainty and security, and that we cannot be rid of it. It is nothing so humanly interesting or spiritually dignified. Most often it is only our lazy habit of deciding the most pregnant issues by signs and tokens instead of looking at the things themselves.

* *Race: A Study in Superstition*, New York, 1937 (Revised edition, Torchbooks, Harper, 1965).

The absolute is commonly nothing more than a penny footrule applied to cases where we need complicated instruments of precision. In the realm of ideas it is a single arbitrary notion used where we need a many-sided concept.[8] True, much of our life is mechanical and we cannot help ourselves. When the light is green, we go. It is convenient, but at a price. There comes a time when by a concourse of circumstances green means danger, and we all rush headlong to disaster. The reverse also holds, and like the little girl in the tale who would not learn to read, we run away from a sign saying "Free Lemonade" because we associate all signs with dangerous bulls. To put it plainly, nine times out of ten we cannot read the signs, which may be why we judge by color, asking: "Is he a Red?" instead of "What is he saying?" All the more reason why, to avoid the fatal reflex action of the Montagues and the Capulets, we must cherish intellectual democracy: we need one another's eyes.

Whatever the dogmatist may feel about it, this relativist, instrumental philosophy is the philosophy of free democracy par excellence; it is rooted in its culture and it stands confirmed by the two great techniques of the human mind which are synonymous with civilization—science and art. Science, of course, we accept as "modern" and useful, but not understanding its bearing (as I shall show) we erect it also into a sinister cast-iron absolute of which racialism is only one manifestation. Simultaneously we neglect the lesson of art. We take it for a pastime of the ivory tower or else for a convenient tool of political propagandists. We forget that it has a function as the organizer of our manifold human desires. In fact we have to be aroused by the follies of Nazis and revolutionist talk to see that art contributes directly to our well-being. Fortunately our democratic practice is often better than our principles: if art and scholarship were entities remote from life, there would have been no point in giving asylum to Einstein and Thomas Mann. If art were the plaything of dilettantes or a conspiracy of highbrows, there would be no need to worry about the alleged decadence of democratic society. Since we do worry about it, we must repel the raids of political propagandists upon the arts, square our daily thinking with our pretensions to civilized life, in short, defend our stake in twentieth-century culture for the sake of that wider culture which is democracy.

3   *Decadence: Fascist or Futurist?*

IN common conversation art is known as a Good Thing,
but in most people that amiable concession vanishes at
the first practical touch. Few will save on a bun to buy a
book, for the majority confuse the practical with the immediate. Nevertheless art is indispensable to civilized
life, art fosters civilization. So much has already been
hinted at, but before going into the far-reaching fascist
theories of art and decadence, I must give a novel reason
or two in behalf of this platitude, lest its familiarity as
an old saw induce the belief that it has lost its teeth. The
man of art, then, is essential to civilization because he
is in fact the Eternal Pragmatist, the born enemy of absolute systems, the champion of mind in its struggle with
matter. The artist seeks to mould materials to his will by
taking advantage of their nature. He works with an un-
wavering eye for the only durable kind of success, and
therefore works at what he is after and not some easier
but irrelevant task next door. The result of his toil, when
it is not a mere comfort or convenience, organizes and
satisfies our emotion, adds to our reality, and fulfills our
creative instinct. This will have to do until Chapter 6.

In the light of these reasons it becomes clear why it
is of the essence of totalitarianism to control art, science,
and thought. Totalitarianism is uniformity, a rigid system forced on life for the sake of an order which democratic nature does not normally present. Art, science,
and the free expression of thought, on the contrary, mir-

29

Of Human Freedom

ror the variety of nature and give it many diverse kinds of order.[1] What ensues is a conflict between the dictators and the culture of the twentieth century. It appears that there is a democratic art which is dangerous and decadent, and fascist counterparts which are worthy and great. Uniformity requires that culture be either pure or purged. Hence the endless preaching about degenerate art, the "race mind," and that monstrous absolute, a politico-national culture.

This is the theory. How does it work? Though we now speak of totalitarianism as a single thing, it so happened that in the heyday of the fascist and communist dictatorships the art advocated and encouraged by one State—Italian Futurism—was the bugaboo of the other. While Marinetti, the founder and expounder of Futurism, enjoyed power and honor at Rome, Hitler could be heard at Nürnberg storming against "this Bolshevist and Futurist art which is an anarchical regression."[2] This slight difference of opinion only shows how difficult it is to obtain a "safe" sort of culture and how careful a dictator must be.

If we try to understand why two identical tyrannies which accused the West of decadence flatly contradicted each other about the cultural symptoms of the disease, we shall also understand why, despite appearances, such theories have really nothing to do with art. We shall see that they are clumsy and desperate political makeshifts. The artistic situation was thus instructive about the doubtfulness of decadence; after which it was only necessary to show the roots and purposes of modernism to show that "this crazy modern art" had an intelligible meaning we should heed.

Nor was it hard to see why Germany should repudiate modern art at the same time that her sister state supported it. For both of them art was a weapon loaded with propaganda and also brandished as a token of superiority.

30

But in Germany, the so-called "modernistic" art akin to Italian futurism was favored before Hitler by the republican regime. Modernist architecture built proletarian housing plans; expressionist paintings filled the public galleries; the "new music" was played in the concert halls. Modernism and the Weimar Republic became linked in the public mind as one movement. A reaction against the government of that era felt bound to attack its art.

In Italy, contrariwise, the modernists led by Marinetti threw in their lot with fascism almost from the start. Moreover, their attack on nineteenth-century academic art and bourgeois taste seemed to parallel Mussolini's attack on nineteenth-century liberalism and bourgeois parliaments. A political accident and a vaguely similar protest against the past resulted in the union of futurism and Italian fascism. Thus all the factors at work were negative. Neither in Germany nor in Italy was there an organic relation between modern forms of art and the new political slogans.

Rather, the same demagogic purpose, but moving in opposite directions, accounted for Mussolini's acceptance and Hitler's denunciation of the alleged decadent art. In Germany the slogan *Keine Kraft ohne Schönbeit* proclaimed the feeling of the common man that beauty is an absolute quality by which modern art can be proved ugly. The famous exhibition of "Degenerate Art"[3] in Munich was based on this feeling and showed how the taste for conventional art can be fused with a politically conditioned response.* The aim was of course perfectly

---

* The show brought forth the paintings—sometimes from the museum's cellars rather than public galleries—dating from the period of "Fulfillment and Reconciliation," while the curators who had bought them were publicly punished. The punishers conveniently forgot that many of the offending pictures had been bought regardless of merit with a view to relieving starving artists after the war. The confusion, again, was political and purposeful.

obvious. It was to insure the German people's associating modernism with Marxism—both perverse, complex, and decadent, Marxism, moreover, is international, like modern art; hence its hatefulness to an absolute, self-sufficing national culture. Once a year, at party rallies, Hitler turned upside down Fichte's slogan: "There is no hope of preserving a cultural Germany without a political Germany." Right or wrong, Germany felt that national union was an all-too-recent fact, still menaced by outside forces. Fichte was fighting Napoleon and the ideas of the French Revolution. Hitler, a hundred and twenty-five years later, still referred to that *furchtbare Erscheinung,*[4] the revolution and Napoleon, and still fought it psychologically.

Whether or not Hitler was genuinely interested in culture makes little difference.* Others since his time have continued to believe in culture as a cement for nationality; and if art can be revolutionary propaganda,† there is no good reason why it should not propagate nationalism as well. Hitler's nationalism was racial as well as cultural, but since race is apparently not a sufficient bond in itself, it must be helped by regimented art and science.‡

In Germany the practical machinery for this pupose was recent. Whereas in France official academic art had been centralized since Richelieu and Louis XIV, it was only after Hitler's seizure of power, in 1934 to be exact, that German theatres, concert halls, and other centres were "coördinated." In the older Germany—that loose confederation of small states—the great number of independent courts fostered much independent art, particularly music. If Bach did not get on at Arnstadt, there was always Mühlhausen; if Liszt and Wagner were booed

* It is said on good authority that foreign offers to buy the alleged degenerate paintings were consistently refused.
† See the next chapter.
‡ The racial interpretation of culture was not confined to Germany and thus demands separate treatment. See Chapter 7.

at Leipzig (where Mendelssohn flourished), there was always Dresden or Weimar. Where could they go under any modern well-planned state?

Centralization offers some advantages, chiefly financial; but so far they have not been used anywhere to great effect. Even academic artists have had a hard time.* The German Ministry of Propaganda was too busy with national unification; the Russian politicans and generals have fumbled in their choices of men and doctrines. Under the Nazis the scheme of *Kraft durch Freude* was meant to break down provincialism by travel through the country in a spirit of fraternity, to an accompaniment of songs, picnics, and nature worship. That was the positive part of the program. The negative part consisted in weeding out politically undesirable intellectuals, playing changes on the myth of race, and creating by repetition a powerful antagonism to certain words—Futurism, Expressionism, Bolshevism, Anarchy, Revolution, Democracy, Individualism, Self-Expression. These hated words merged into the great creed of anti-modernism, a creed shaped to fit current political difficulties and having nothing to do with art itself, with democracy, or with decadence.

2

The disquieting thing about anti-modernism in 1939 was that it was not limited to Germany. Many who were not Nazis or communists, but Catholics, liberals, or classicists, believed in the fact of decadence.[5] Many Americans besides those that fell into these groups likewise damned the whole modern movement in art, on the ground of its unintelligibility.

When one looked into the complaints, the unanimity

---

* Liebermann, the one-time master of German academic painting, was for a while made much of by officialdom in opposition to the modernists, but even before his death he became *persona non grata*.

disappeared. The communists said that it was capitalism that lay dying, hence art should take its inspiration from the live forces of revolution. Others said that it was democracy and the liberal tradition that were decadent. Art must go back to national or racial ideals and make a wider popular appeal than modernism. The Neo-Catholics and anti-Romanticists of every hue also demanded a "return to the old rules"—they were thinking of Greek and Roman art, Aristotle, and Saint Thomas—and they prayed for a culture that would combine the critical tenets of classicism, as T. S. Eliot urged, with Anglo-Catholicism in religion and royalism in politics. All groups united again at the first opportunity to condemn, and, without choosing or distinguishing among the manifold products of modernism, intoned the triple anathema: "Anarchy, Decadence, Lunacy!"

That union on culture was temporary and perhaps superficial, for it concealed many different ideas. It passed judgment of different kinds, but because these judgments were alike all unfavorable they were taken for identical. What permitted this confusion among false allies was the ambiguity of the words "modern" and "modernistic," no less than the very real difficulty of the subject itself.

For some—and to this day—modern art goes back to the Impressionists in painting and music and to the Symbolists in literature.* One frequently sees in a shop that sells so-called "modernistic" furniture a reproduction of a Monet painted in 1880. The two may go well enough together, but the purchaser and the merchant appear to think that the two styles are contemporary. In the twentieth century names and styles are still harder for the public to place. In painting alone there are Cubists, Futurists, Abstractionists, Expressionists, Dadaists, and Surrealists. Individual artists make their mark erratically

* Say: Debussy and Ravel, Cézanne and Van Gogh, Rimbaud and Ibsen, Proust and Henry James.

during their career or after their death: Van Gogh comes to general notice simultaneously with Picasso, his junior by twenty-five years. Add to all this the complexity of the art itself and it is no wonder that those who decried modernism said first that it was worthless, and second that it reflected chaos.

Clearly, even if totalitarian theory is disqualified by its motives, one must make up one's mind about the imputed chaos. Where does it really lie—in the facts, in the catchwords, or in oneself? A canvas more or less may not matter, but our share in the world's history and our sanity as a social group do matter, to say nothing of our possible enjoyment. Even when "accepted," modernism may still hold back painful disclosures.

Futurism, to take the word most often used as a synonym of chaos, is obviously a misnomer. No art can be an art of the future, except in the sense that its contemporaries do not recognize its merits and the artist hopes future generations will. Futurism was from the outset an art of the present, an aspect of modernism which no one who is not a picture dealer or an art historian need differentiate from cognate movements. It is much more important to grasp two great facts about modernism as a whole: one, that the adjective "modern," in its special, historical meaning, can only refer to ideas and works of art produced since 1900 (and even more strictly to ideas and works that show a break with Symbolism and Impressionism); and the other, that the main directions and techniques of modernism were all laid down and exemplified before the Great War. The significance of these time limits is that modernism is not a hangover from 1890 preciosity, nor an expression of moral decadence following a big war. Its great constructive lines were laid down between 1900 and 1915.[6]

So much for chronology. Anti-modernism is wont to make other charges which so nearly resemble Hitler's own that it is hard to know which is the disciple of whom. Modern art, said the Führer, is international and materialistic. It is the pastime of the homeless and the foot-loose; it is a hoax perpetrated by people who are technically untrained and by charlatans who swindle the public. It bears no more valid relation to the present-day world than it does to traditional work. The very principle of modernism is folly, he argued, because it supposes that originality grows on every bush, and that a new modernism can appear every ten years in defiance of stylistic continuity.

This last point is typical in its ignoring of facts. Anyone who takes the trouble to study the output of a modernist who has attained ripe years soon discovers in his works a normal continuity of artistic attitude. Changes of manner may well be found, as in the works of Picasso and Schönberg, but if Shakespeare is granted his four periods and Beethoven his three styles, there is no reason on earth for restricting our contemporary creators to a lesser number of changes, changes which in fact correspond to the maturing of the man far more than to any striving for novelty in the artist.

Continuity, it must be remembered, is like Order, a structure which the historian half discovers in the facts, half imposes on their confusion after the event. Nor is it surprising that this order should be hidden to the contemporaries, especially to-day when democracy has vastly increased the number of those who think themselves artists.

The public also has increased and has become more demanding. It now wants art to be backed up by "theory" either of a social or of a philosophic cast, and it judges the art as much by the theory as by the work itself. All this contributes to the "chaos," which is not much cleared up by the professional critics, swamped as they are with names, dates, schools, and works. Few have the time to organize their thoughts or thoroughly survey the field. The chaos therefore has its roots in the outer world but it remains in our heads. Time will take care of it, though not perhaps so wisely as one thinks. Of the millions of books and canvases only thousands will remain, and of those thousands a handful will shine after the tumult dies.[7] Posterity, seeing a much simplified panorama, will see order where we see chaos.

3

As for the substantive relation of modern art to the present, politicians abroad and non-artists anywhere are certainly disingenuous when they complain of a chaotic art which is also "escapist." Some modern art takes chaos as its subject, but it takes it in the modern world, which is presumably our own handiwork. We may not like to see it again in art, but in that case the charge of "escape" is false. Surrealism, Dadaism and their sequels, for example, reflected the First World War; they came at the tail end of modernism as a joke upon it and upon themselves. If they went in for the fantastic and gruesome—like those good Nordics Dürer and Holbein—it was precisely because the men of action had provided them with excellent subject matter. The wonder is that in such an anarchical world there should be so much highly organized and deeply thought-out art: in Joyce and Dos Passos; in Van Dieren, Schönberg, and Varèse; in Franz Marc, Braque, Gleizes, and the great architects of Europe and America.

The principles and techniques of modern art, it cannot be too often repeated, antedate the first war. They were devised and developed to satisfy very precise artistic needs, in the full knowledge of past traditions. The new artists were not pandering to a "fad for modernism" when they began: no such thing as modernism existed. They began, like most creators, with the world indifferent or hostile to their efforts. The fads that followed ten or fifteen years later, after the war, are a fifth-hand effect of their work—the common distortion which follows any novelty and which proves nothing either for or against it.

What led the moderns to innovate in the first place was the pressure of a world-wide phenomenon; namely, the twentieth-century phase of the industrial revolution. The new impressions and effects of space, time, and number in human experience; the great speeds and large masses; the sudden elevation into the air, instantaneous communication, and new materials—these things revolutionized the arts by substituting what amounts to a new sensory world for the old, breaking down old forms and forcing the artists to build new ones.

This is not the place to "prove" that this psychological change explains every last item of modernism; it can only be proposed as the clue to what unites the productions of the modern school—say the work of Brancusi the sculptor, Mary Wigman the dancer, and Frank Lloyd Wright the architect. The common element transcends their individual styles and not only disposes of the charge that they are charlatans, but likewise refutes the political or dilettante absolutists by showing that modern art is the twin of modern science. If the one is decadent, so is the other; if we want to save ourselves by more modern science and less superstition, we must also have more modern art and less absolutism.

It is of course the awareness of this bond with science that inspires the cry of materialism.[8] Modern art is accused of destroying spiritual values. When anyone says this, he is either playing on words or misrepresenting the nature of art from ignorance or prejudice. Machine civilization has produced new materials offering many new possibilities to the plastic artist, musician, and architect. The desire to exploit new possibilities is the oldest tradition in the world; a truth of which the heads of Propaganda Ministries can easily assure themselves by visiting the cave paintings of Cro-Magnon man or reading Vasari's *Lives of the Eminent Painters, Sculptors and Architects.*

If it is the "hard" and "abstract" element in modernism that is meant by materialism, the argument answers itself: abstraction is the antithesis of sensuality or crassness. In any case it is a mistake to suppose that the "idealization" held to be the mark of past art has given place to a grosser realism due to industrial worldliness. Art is always organization, modern art most of all precisely because it has to deal with a harsh, noisy, crowded, many-layered life. That is why we cannot as democrats disown modern art in order to have the pleasure of refuting the totalitarian critique. We must on the contrary take the offensive by showing that any other kind of art shirks the realities of the mechanized life now prevailing as the common culture.

A final meaning of materialism which is used to discredit modern art is that of philosophical materialism, a theory associated with Marxist socialism. Marxism, in turn, is (or has been) the creed of many modern artists. One is thus free to jump to the conclusion that all modern art is materialistic ("no idealism"), that all "noisy music" and "difficult poetry" is Marxist—at least in the West. This kind of logic is no doubt what qualifies the absolutist politician for the post of cultural mentor. Quite apart from the fact that many modernists, such as T. S. Eliot, are anti-Marxists, the philosophy of Marxism is no more the efficient cause of Rivera or Gorky's art than the smell of rotten apples is that of

39

Schiller's poetry.* The artist's tastes and views are not the *cause,* but only a condition, of his art. The artist is almost always a dramatist: he sees life in the round, and he paints the "proletarian loaf of bread" not because he has read Karl Marx but because he feels the reality of the poor man's loaf and has the ability to convey his sense of it.

When Hitler combated modernism because it was international he was at last in harmony with the facts. The modern architecture he attacked *is* international. It is the work of the American Louis Sullivan, the Frenchman Auguste Perret, the Austrian Otto Wagner, and a host of other Europeans of every nationality. This does not mean that the German *Bauhaus* was not at the same time truly German, if by nationality in art we mean the associations of authorship and local adaptation. The great artists who are now touted as preëminently German—Goethe, Wagner, Nietzsche—are Germans to be sure, but they are no spontaneous outcroppings of the German soil. Soil is never enough for art; there has got to be Mind, and that immediately implies other minds in countless number and remote places, who bring their gifts to any great artist or work of art. To maintain that any personality or style, in a civilization such as ours, can be home-grown and free from foreign influences is simply not true to fact, and the nation that tries to make it so will shortly find its culture turning imitative, anemic, headed for death.

The best proof of what I am saying was to be found in the Paris World's Fair of 1937. Indeed, though the fact escaped notice, the Exhibition was a test of politically stimulated art. The three great dictatorships—Russia and Germany face to face, and Italy near by—

---

* Goethe tells us how he accidentally discovered that his fellow poet could not compose without half opening a desk drawer which he kept full of overripe apples. See G. H. Lewes, *Life of Goethe.*

were obviously bent on showing the world what they could do in the way of culture. German machinery, as usual, easily surpassed the rest in boldness of design and fineness of materials. But the buildings were commonplace and the fine-arts exhibits were dull to the point of depravity. The paintings of Stalin and his generals, and of a Russian battleship crew watching a performance of *Carmen* on deck, might have been daubed by an academic third-rater a hundred years ago. Moreover one had to look twice to be sure that Stalin and his gold-braided aides were not the Tsar and his staff. The busts of Lenin and other revolutionary leaders were equally pallid, and only the Hitler iconography across the way could reach greater depths of artistic ineptitude.

The Italian paintings, thanks to the acceptance of Futurism, showed more modern intentions. Severini, who is a gifted man,* contributed a few decorative pieces, but the compromise modernism of the rest betrayed the timidity of the artist who looks over his shoulder at the master of his soul and fate. The sculpture chiefly portrayed Mussolini and the complementary glories of war and maternity. On the whole, although Italian art was definitely trying to be modern with government backing, the results were feeble. Nothing shown seemed comparable in freshness and vigor to the panels by Gleizes, Jacques Villon, and Delaunay in the French aviation building; or to numerous mural designs and decorations in the scores of other pavilions.

In one respect, however,—and this deeply concerns the "decadent" democracies,—Russia, Italy, and Germany were thoroughly modern, completely successful, and virtually identical. The huge photographs on the

---

* He won the Quadrennial Prize of 100,000 lire in 1935, though his post-war canvases had not the vigor of his early work done in Paris before 1914. The timidity which results from political dictation is but a worse degree of the fault produced by academies.

walls depicting scenes of the new national life were a revelation of modernism and art. All the devices of camera angle, enlargement, distortion, and mass effects —all of them direct outgrowths of the prohibited Cubism and Expressionism—were used to give without any overt preaching an impression of collective strength and technological modernity appropriate for nations that profess to command the future.

In these photographs utility had brushed aside prejudice, and national pride was bringing out aspects of life in ways which are officially forbidden the artist. Since we who believe in democracy have also tended in the past to damn the artist and accept the photograph, we may like to think that it is the machine, the camera, that is ruining art. Like most accusations against the machine the suggestion is foolish. Behind the machine there is always a man, even when one doubts in which of the two the brains reside. The machine never acts by itself, and when the man begins to behave like one, the suspension of his intelligence is often due to an outside compulsion. Under tyranny it is the dictator's politics; elsewhere, it is some other absolute, social, national, or partisan. No wonder the culture maker succumbs. The masses prefer their old favorites; academic taste attacks him for being newfangled; nationalists object to his foreign decadence; and now the dictator, understanding only what the populace might like to assail, sentences his style and his neck for treason to Idealism and the State.

4

In attacks on modernism and loose talk of decadence, the danger to democracy is at once plain and insidious. First and foremost the artist is in danger. But the common mind is also at the mercy of the new ready-made culture, through which may be disseminated every kind of moral turpitude. Lacking faith in modernism—the art that grew from spontaneous desire and within which we can still freely choose—we are the sport of vulgar suggestion and incitement to fanaticism. The common assault on modern art by communists and other totalitarians is a warning. It expresses a political disappointment and a political impatience. To hear the totalitarian critics, steadily echoed among us, art is serious, art is social, art is all-important.[9] But few are really interested in what art does for the inner life of the individual or the group. They are all interested in what art could or should do as propaganda, as reassurance, or as a claim to the honor and envy of other groups. Hitler wanted modern art to look just like the art of Germany's great period; Russia still wants modern art to be "social realism," that is, to enhance the political and social actuality as an ad enhances the product on sale, Mussolini wanted art to stiffen the morale of the Italians; the Anglo-Catholics wanted modern art to bolster up Order and Religion. The implication is that individually or collectively we are always on parade and what we want from art is a façade.

In this pseudo-practical view of art its true practicality is forgotten. A false dilemma is thrust in our face, whereby if art does not strengthen our façade or encourage our fellow man, it must be "escapist" and "precious." And by a final mischance, those who are indifferent equally to art and to politics also object to modern art, because it is *not* sufficiently remote and escapist. They want modern art to be charming or frivolous or at any rate unlike the reality of the modern world.[10]

In a sheltered academic nook the theorists of Classicism, yearning for a serene absence of care, project their wish into a past where it never existed. They smooth out history and overlook the "chaos" of the past, classic or romantic. They abuse Rousseau, Revolution, and

Romanticism, from which, according to them, all forms of modernism and social ills are descended. Everybody is looking for scapegoats; it saves thinking.

In these conditions it is a trifle premature to say that we have no great artists and that the modern, democratic, liberal culture is decadent. Decadence is a reproachful and not a descriptive world. It implies the loss of a sense of direction, but takes it for granted that art should be directed by the critic, the politician, or the Philistine rather than the artist. If decadent meant something to the purpose, one could say with as much justice that modern art is vigorous and that its audience is decadent—fallen from grace—for it is too full of irrelevant notions, of doctrinaire suspicions, and of fear of its own times to keep its eyes open to art.

This view seems supported by the fact that in the thoroughly modern arts of photography, advertising, and motion pictures, adjustment and appreciation have long since come about. The absence of "ideology" in these commercial arts authorized novelty and dramatic distortion where the painter's eye or poet's ear producing the same effects is declared incomprehensible. Modernism is in truth neither Marxist nor anarchical, neither barbaric nor decadent. Hitler is in the end our best witness on the point. With grandiloquent and sweeping absolutes—nationalism, race, idealism, beauty —he assailed bolshevism and Futurism, but his photographic propaganda was indistinguishable from that of the Futurists on his right and the communists on his left. He had to swallow and even to use modernism, though he continued mouthing his "principles," saying: *"Dieser Staat soll nicht eine Macht sein ohne Kultur,"* adding as by a happy afterthought—*"und keine Kraft ohne Schönheit."**

* "This state shall not be a power without culture, nor is there strength without beauty." From his Culture-Day Speech at Nürnberg, September 1936.

44

4 *The Myth of Revolutionary Culture*

THE defenders of democracy in our midst are ready to repudiate the totalitarian ways of treating art when they emanate from fascist countries, but they make an exception in favor of dictatorial absolutes that seem to support revolution. Revolutionary culture is felt to be worthier than bourgeois culture, and there is much talk to urge the making of such a culture in places where revolution is not yet in progress or even in prospect. In some quarters this advocacy has become dogmatic and dangerous to question, though one might have supposed it would fail under the strain of its inconsistency: if great art is materially conditioned and can avoid bourgeois decadence only by being born of revolution, what hope is there for any self-styled revolutionary art in bourgeois countries like the United States? What is, in fact, a revolutionary work of art and how shall we tell it from a mere by-product of "bourgeois decadence"?

Diego Rivera used to tell us that even a painting of a loaf of bread by Cézanne will reflect the character of the revolutionary artist.[1] If so, the influence of revolution in art must be very subtle. Others have maintained that "art is a weapon in the class struggle,"[2] which suggests propaganda rather than subtlety. In the criticism of the social philosophers it is usual to find the great artists of the past classified and judged according to their revolutionary or counter-revolutionary tendency. From Shakespeare to Goethe and from Balzac to Henry

James, the world's literature has been combed for evidence, and among more recent figures, Sartre, Juenger, Pasternak, and others have been put into one camp or the other by turns, which shows that a correct diagnosis is not easy to make.[3]

"Revolutionary" has in the process become a term of critical praise or blame, but its meaning continues dark. The reviewer of a dance recital once questioned whether the performer's movements were revolutionary or merely bourgeois. Prokoviev had a difficult time with official censors of his melodic idiom, and some unspecified element in an opera earned Shostakovitch an official rebuke.[4] Chord progressions seem no safer than loaves of bread from the influence of something that one finds often invoked but not defined. Is there in fact a meaning to be found? Taking all possible cases, revolutionary art must be either art by revolutionists, art for revolutionists, or art about revolutionists.* The first would mean almost anything produced by a certain group of people; art for revolutionists amounts to doctrine or propaganda conveyed through art; while art about revolutionists must be criticism dealing with social problems, regardless of the author or his point of view.

Social today is translated into proletarian. But "proletarian" itself is ambiguous. "Proletarian art," "art for the masses," "the ideology of the proletariat," are common phrases suggesting that proletarian and revolutionist are synonymous. This is patently untrue and it is this confusion of terms that makes it difficult for the critic to say whether Jules Romains, for instance, is a revolutionary or a fascist. "Proletarian" can only signify a member of the proletariat, a class of society set off by its economic status, membership in which implies nothing about political beliefs and less than nothing about culture. The

* The "revolutionizing" of technique in art is another matter, which I deal with below, pp. 58–59.

critic who wants to come to grips with reality must take "revolutionary" to mean a state of mind, and forget "proletarian," which means a state of pocketbook.

That the state of pocket may influence the state of mind is true, but it is not an inescapable influence: Marx and Lenin were bourgeois with revolutionary minds. Art is the product of minds, and although the minds are attached to bodies and both are formed by the society in which they live, when we want a poem or a portrait or a song we address ourselves to minds and not to bodies with untrained minds, or to indefinite "social conditions" and "means of production." So true is this that revolutionary critics have again and again tried to show that great artists in the past were great in proportion as their minds were moulded by revolutionary ideas. The instance which is always brought up is that of Wordsworth, who is supposed to have written great poetry when he was a sympathizer with the French Revolution and to have gone dry and prosaic when he became a conservative.[5]

This view assumes that a revolutionary movement by its freshness, vigor, and high-mindedness will inspire great art, while an outworn and corrupt system of society can only produce lifeless copies of old models. It asks us to consider, not only the poem or symphony, but also the opinions of the author. Is the correlation valid? The Wordsworth example is an unlucky one. So far from any connection between revolution and great poetry obtaining in his case, the very reverse is true. By 1798 Wordsworth and Coleridge were well on the road to disillusionment and repudiation of the French Revolution, and it was between 1796 and 1798 that the first *Lyrical Ballads* were written. Before the earlier date Wordsworth's work was imitative and unimportant. It would be easy to show likewise that Wordsworth's later years, with increasing Toryism, were by no

47

means devoid of great poetry—nor were Coleridge's of great ideas. For both of them the abandonment of a narrow (and revolutionary) rationalism patterned on Godwin and Tom Paine meant, understandably enough, the opening up of the sluices of emotional power and the writing of great poetry.

To be sure, a single instance one way or the other proves nothing. The revolutionary critic need not give up, but he had better revise his proofs. Besides, the reading of the facts in the Wordsworth example is absurdly literal. It supposes that events and ideas have cultural effects only while they are going on, like an electric current that ceases to give light when it is switched off. This is tantamount to saying that a poet can write love poems only while he is actively in love, which is notoriously false. Wordsworth's own definition of poetry as emotion recollected in tranquillity applies here to remind us that there are after-effects of a love affair or a revolution.

Within the last three hundred years Western Europe has undergone two great revolutionary upheavals: the French Revolution of 1789 and the English Puritan Revolution of 1642. If we limit ourselves to the two decades more or less that each took to work itself out, and look for the distinctive culture of these periods, what do we find? We find a great quantity of art, an immense amount of printed and painted stuff, of songs and plays, and a goodly number of potential creators; but we are forced to report that neither era produced any body of art or thought that we value to-day.

This verdict at first seems too severe: what about *Paradise Lost* and *Pilgrim's Progress*? What about Byron, Beethoven, Shelley, and the French romanticists? The dates answer inexorably: the great bulk of what we tend to associate with revolution came either before or after, came during the time of pre-revolutionary "decadence" or during the triumph of the counter-revolution. Even so, the feeling is strong that there must be some loophole, some flaw in the argument. Great movements, whatever their motives, must have left cultural traces. Is it that we have overestimated the greatness of these two revolutions, or that its leaders lacked a proper appreciation of art?

These suppositions will not bear scrutiny. Both Puritanism and the French revolutionary idealism spread to the ends of the world with a speed appropriate to the existing means of communication; and their leaders actively sought to foster a distinctive culture. The French revolutionists loudly denied that they were a "republic of Visigoths" and boasted that they were "a nation resplendent with culture and enlightenment." True, the old culture was repudiated as the work of men who worked for the court and nobility, just as revolutionary artists to-day accuse their colleagues of pandering to bourgeois tastes. The French called for a *style révolutionné*[6] and a poetry addressed to the taste of all the citizens, like ancient Greek drama.

One of the notable results of this attitude was the entirely novel spectacle of the *fêtes du peuple* with the music, poetry, and ritual provided by anoymous or now obscure artists. Nowadays we hardly know the existence of these popular works; nor are the modern critics thinking of outdoor festivals with their ephemeral artistry when they speak of culture arising from the Revolutionary Idea. They mean important works by great artists. The poet André Chénier fulfills their requirement better. He was a true poet, keen to sense the spirit of the times, and eager to leave a great "scientific-political epic." But the practical revolutionists cut off his head, and the lyric masterpiece he has left us, *La Jeune Captive,* reflects a sympathy not indeed with the counter-revolution, but with an innocent and noble-born victim of the Terror.

As in our day, the theatre reflected the trend of the

French revolutionary ideas, but the modern educated
man can rarely name a single title from the enormous
quantity of plays written and produced in the period.
He may perhaps have heard of one—the very bad
libretto of Beethoven's *Fidelio,* which is a German adaptation of Bouilly's *Léonore, or Conjugal Love.* Patriotism, virtue, and the hatred of tyrants are its familiar
motifs. The characters are puppets, the style is flat, and
the conflict mechanical. It may be objected that the play
is poor because Bouilly was a wretched writer,[7] and that
is indeed the principal cause; but when we look at the
other dramas of the period we see that *Léonore* is both
typical and of relatively high merit. The titles of the
common output suffice to give the show away:—

Opéra-Comique National—*The Civic Festival,* a
  comedy in five acts
Théâtre National—*The Victory at Marathon or
  the Triumph of Liberty,* an heroic drama in
  four acts
Théâtre du Vaudeville—*Morning and Evening in
  the Village. The Divorce. Union in the Vil-
  lages*
Théâtre du Lycée des Arts—*The Return of the
  National Fleet*
Théâtre de la République—*Divorce among the
  Tartars,* a comedy in five acts
Théâtre Français—*Buzot, King of Calvados*[8]

Three themes—patriotism, popular virtue, and hatred
of kings and priests—are played on with a revolting
monotony and a desperate unimaginativeness. The scenes
and props are all the same: oubliettes, prison cells, and
virtuous village greens. The characters are oversimpli-
fied types, some of them, like Chauvin (the spiritual
father of Chauvinism), apparently true to life but infinitely boring. Their attributes are as inescapable as

our modern race characteristics. All monks are lecherous, all aristocrats are traitors, all wealthy bourgeois are ambitious and hypocritical. Poverty equals simplicity equals sanctity. On this pattern Molière's *Misanthrope* was reworked by the politician and dramatic critic Fabre d'Eglantine so that Alceste became a true-blue republican and Philinte an odious aristocrat.

Surely the *Figaro* comedies written in the decadent era by the alleged cynic "de" Beaumarchais (*né* Pierre Caron) were more nearly revolutionary as well as more entertaining. And on the serious side, the great drama of revolutionary politics itself, no piece of the period can compare with Büchner's *Death of Danton*, written in reactionary Germany in the early 1830's.

The music is on a par with the drama. With the exception of a few pieces by Gossec and Méhul, the contents of collections like the *Chansonnier de la Montagne* —one among hundreds—are distressingly banal. The one great musical creation of the revolution is Rouget de Lisle's *Marseillaise*,* a single lyrical outburst transcending the personality of its author, who could never rekindle the fire of his genius, but (in his own words to Berlioz) "smouldered on with a fire of straw."[9]

Out of the *Marseillaise* Gardel made a ballet, but it failed. The people preferred to dance themselves rather than see dancing. The *Carmagnole,* taken from an Italian fertility dance, gave them the music, just as the streets gave them locale, without cost. The quadrille and the minuet were of course banned as aristocratic, and the ballet (though it is said to have been Stalin's favorite form of art) was both too expensive and too reminiscent of courtliness. But after the Terror over a thousand dance halls were opened in Paris and were allowed to

* The French Communists have been known to hiss the *Marseillaise,* because it is a reactionary, patriotic, nationalist anthem. From 1804 to 1830 it was banned as a revolutionary song. What is it intrinsically?

stay open seven nights a week as a relief measure for overstrained nerves.

No better word can be said for the plastic arts. Apart from David's sketches of people going to the guillotine, there is virtually no live painting or sculpture. David's combined classical and republican ardor paradoxically froze his great talents just as the theme of civic virtue killed the drama. Gros and Géricault are patriotic painters of the Empire, not the Revolution. Delacroix is still to come, as is Rude, whose sculpture of the Volunteers of 1792 on one of the sides of the Arc de Triomphe is the true expression of revolutionary fervor, but dated forty years after the event.

The philosophers and scientists of the period are the *Idéologues*, led by Cabanis and Destutt de Tracy, whose fame has been obscured, precisely owing to the Terror and the Napoleonic censorship. While the nation was piously worshiping the State, the Supreme Being, and Robespierre, the Ideologues were working at physiology and abnormal psychology. They were called materialists and atheists and were intermittently debarred from meeting or doing research until 1830. As for physical science, when the great chemist Lavoisier, who was condemned to death by the Revolutionary Tribunal, asked for time to finish some experiments, he was told—so runs the anecdote—"The Republic has no need of scientists."

2

The English Puritan Revolution dealt with art even more consistently than the French. The Long Parliament ordered the destruction of church organs and the closing of all theatres for purely political and propagandistic reasons. The courtly emptiness and obscenity of the theatre were apparent long before the revolution, and the "puritanical" cloture of September 2, 1642, showed in fact a typically modern attitude towards "decadent art." Surreptitious performances continued and masques or "droll humours" were given here and there, but the period of interdiction, as might be expected, produced nothing new.[10]

The attitude of Puritans like Milton, Cromwell, and Andrew Marvell—all of whom were devotees of music and the fine arts—was dictated by entirely revolutionary considerations: they renounced art out of devotion to the political cause. The thought of the revolutionists was to be "practical." The Old Testament was preferred to the New because it gave better authority for the stern reformatory attitude and placed less insistence on forgiveness and charity. As in present-day revolutionary movements, the cultured man—Milton, Marvell, or Fox —felt he must consecrate himself to immediate tasks which preclude artistic creation.

The theological form in which the Puritans put this belief has incidentally obscured the importance of their revolution in the eyes of modern revolutionists. Marxism, being anticlerical and "scientific," takes it for granted that Milton and Cromwell were as benighted as "the superstitious masses." As a matter of fact, the zeal of the various Puritan sects was much closer to modern economic-mindedness than was the French Revolution. Robespierre had no clear grasp of economic problems and was a parliamentarian before being a dictator; whereas the seventeenth-century groups held strong economic views. The Anabaptists were communists; the Ranters were anarchists; the Levelers and Diggers were collectivists; the Fifth Monarchy Men were totalitarians. One Leveler, Colonel Rainborow, declared in General Council, "Sir, I see that it is impossible to have liberty but all property must be taken away. . . . If it be laid down for a rule and if you will say it, it must be so. But I would fain know what the soldier has fought for all this while. He hath fought to enslave himself, to give power to men of riches, men of estates, to make him a perpetual slave."[11]

In all this controversy, there is much fervor and little art. Milton's *Areopagitica* and Jeremy Taylor's *Discourse of the Liberty of Prophesying* are both pleas for free discussion in a time when freedom was thought impolitic. They are reactions against the revolutionary spirit. Marvell's and Milton's political verse matches in quality the few lyrics of the Cavalier poets on the King's side, and together they form the sum total of poetry for the period. Sir Thomas Browne wrought his prose, and Herrick his pastorals, away from the tumult and without influence from it or upon it. For the rest, the epoch is barren and we must wait until the restoration of the Stuarts to see the renascence of the arts. It was in a Restoration jail that Bunyan wrote *Pilgrim's Progress;* it was in disgrace under the Restoration that Milton composed *Paradise Lost* and *Samson Agonistes;* likewise during the Restoration that Butler wrote *Hudibras* and George Fox did his best work. Newton and Christopher Wren; Purcell, the greatest English musician; Defoe the novelist; Clarendon the historian; Etherege, Wycherley, and Congreve, the dramatists—all belong to the post-revolutionary flowering, a flowering that took place under a regime of religious inquisition and courtly immorality.

3

The record seems clear: what are the tenable conclusions to be drawn from it? The first is chronological. Between 1640 and 1660 in England and between 1789 and 1815 in France, a violent change occurs in public taste. The new revolutionary taste scorns the artificial and formal, associating it with the aristocratic and corrupt. It adopts the simple, the earnest, the puritanical, as its esthetic canons. A large quantity of works is pro-

54

duced, but only a very few—the minor works of great men and the single works of minor artists—emerge from the rubbish. The two post-revolutionary periods, on the other hand, are unusually rich in great men and great works. Can we conclude that counter-revolution inspires better art than does revolution? The answer is no, for two reasons:—

First, an artist who comes to maturity in a time of revolution occasionally manages to live beyond it to produce his masterpiece. That was true of Milton as it was of Chateaubriand, but the date of a man's birth and the "ideology" of the period when he produced great art are not in themselves the cause of his creativeness. They are at most two of the many *conditions* surrounding the event, be it creativeness or sterility. We can say that the two Restoration periods seem to have provided conditions not more favorable, but less unfavorable, to culture than the time of revolution itself. In other words, there was *some* freedom for the men of science and art. But the reactionary phase (and this is the second reason) is not divorced from its forerunner. The Revolution, by its violence and rapid changes, makes a clean sweep of old forms, old reputations, old modes, and thus provides, intellectually speaking, a level plain on which new ideas and new forms can grow. This is an inestimable service; but the flowering depends on the continued presence of gifted men; Chénier and Lavoisier cannot function without their heads. By any political logic Milton and Bunyan should have been killed after the Restoration. *Pilgrim's Progress* would then have been nipped in the bud, and *Paradise Lost* been lost indeed.* The Restoration, if it lets the revolutionists live, even though in jails or in disgrace, does more for art than the

* It is an acknowledged miracle that Milton should have escaped death as a regicide in 1660. Would such an error of omission be possible to-day? Efficiency forbid!

revolution, for the revolution must *absolutely* silence its opponents and control its sympathizers.

The French Revolution, the Puritan—any revolution —is an emergency, a crisis easier to ride than to guide. The political mind must rule, and it works on the self-evident fact that nobody wants art or philosophy during a violent upheaval, any more than an army wants a love tune when going into battle. When it is not merely impertinent, art is rightly felt to be disturbing and dangerous. The only thing that can redeem art in the eyes of the practical revolutionists is that it can be used as political propaganda.

During the French Revolution, all the proposals, measures, and speeches that had to do with education, the theatre, and the arts fell into two classes: censoring, prohibiting, and burning; or else preaching, indoctrinating, and disseminating. Lanthenas in 1793 wanted to build huge auditoriums where audiences could be taught to "feel the delicious sentiment of the People's Majesty." The Jacobin Club considered using balloons to scatter its literature. There was nothing backward about the methods of, or the devotion to, revolutionary culture.

Why then did those men not achieve such a culture? The answer is that they did; but we do not like it, we do not read it; we rightly account it trash. We do not like it because it is not a free culture, because revolution, as Robespierre said, is a system. Systems require absolute, literal propaganda, and absolute literalism is the antithesis of art. To contend that all art is propaganda is to use a partial and misleading truth. All art is propaganda in the sense that it vividly sets forth a man's view of life; and since the times are always more or less out of joint, most artists are critics of life and propagandists for their own beliefs. All art is *not* propaganda in the sense that it contains a political or other doctrine of which someone else has worked out the de-

tails.* A work of art need take sides only with itself and
need not exclude doubts, contradictions, and opposite
sympathies. But a good piece of propaganda must do
just that, for blunt appeals to simple emotions are the
quickest means of moving masses of men.

In its implications, the simplest work of art is complex; the most intricate piece of propaganda is simple.
The desire behind a work of art is to be faithful to a
total perception of reality; the desire behind propaganda
is to achieve at all costs some immediate end. This radical divergence between the aims of art and of propaganda is the best reason why a revolution is unproduc-
tive in its own day.

A second reason surely lies in the machinery whereby
art is forced to serve as "a weapon in the struggle."
Political truths have to be conveyed through the artist
to the public, and the vote of a committee or the decision of a dictator must find quick and broad embodiment. One might as well expect an actor who does not
know his lines to say convincingly what the prompter
whispers to him in small bits. But is it not possible
that the artist, without prompting, will be a born revolutionist? Possibly, but political realities are shifting
things. What is true to-day is false to-morrow, or rather
what is politic to-day is impolitic to-morrow; and about
either "truth" there may be disagreement and misunderstanding. The revolutionary artist-politician is in a
perpetual doubt, one eye on his canvas and the other
on the newspaper. He risks his life or liberty with every
line he puts down and yet has no share in deciding the
policies for which he may suffer. If he is in the government, like Milton, he has no time to be an artist as well,
and the combination of artist and politician is as bad
for culture as the combination of artist and business-
man required by the capitalist system. In neither case

* Even Dante is not orthodox.

does the artist receive any advantage for long-matured creations.

Moreover, the uncertainty about what is virtuous or orthodox leads to a kind of competitive bidding whereby the crudest mind, the stupidest idea, invariably outdoes the finer in "effectiveness." The appalling plays of the French Revolution are one long proof of the fact.

Still other factors conspire to kill art and, occasionally, the artist. The language of art, in spite of all we may like to believe otherwise, is a special tongue understood by relatively few.* Its meaning lies behind the words or canvas and not on the surface. Those empowered to control art during revolution are accustomed to look at the surface of words; indeed are compelled to do so by Philistine public opinion—whence the fate of art. And since revolutions recognize the fact that art deals with life, the work of the musician or sculptor, no less than of the writer or painter, is fair game for the censor. The result is a new kind of academicism which operates by caprice or magic. No one knows in what mysterious way the Grand Inquisitor discovers that certain shapes or sounds are revolutionary and others not. But the mystery does not keep him from deciding just when a statute means treason and when revolutionary counterpoint reaches the counter-revolutionary point. The history of criticism shows how many interpretations of a work of art are possible, and the multitude of parts in such a work permits the determined censor to "prove" anything he has a mind to. Shifting opinions concerning the "revolutionary contents" of Proust, Goethe, and others demonstrate again this commonplace of criticism.

If in calmer moments the adjective "revolutionary" be applied to technique, then the confusion becomes hopeless. The works that have, as we say, revolutionized

* See next chapter.

the technique of any art are few and far between, and they have generally called forth universal condemnation for their "ugliness," "incorrectness," and "modernity." There is no reason for supposing that a great revolutionary leader, or a committee of such leaders, would be any more discerning about technical originality than the average critic. Indeed, the artist who should be inspired to innovate because revolution aims at making all things new would probably meet an aggravated fate: the charge would be, Disturbing the Public Mind and Fiddling While Rome Burns—and it would be true. Here are men dying for humanity and Mr. John Milton argues for the use of blank verse rather than rhyme; M. Claude Monet thinks he prefers a divided palette. As for Citizen Lavoisier, he is weighing the air. Could frivolity go farther?

4

The absolutist who loves art and revolution with equal fervor probably feels that although the facts are convincing, a superior reason of state bids him disregard them. Meanwhile the "anti-red" or merely conservative absolutist on the other side feels vindicated, because he, at least, is for saving culture. The true democrat will avoid the trap of vanity in either case and keep his eye on the practical import of the cultural facts. Whatever may happen in the brain of a critic with a system, art in real life gets produced anyhow, without regard to definitions, doctrines, or even traditions. All of these, however, including the powerful critic's pet system, help determine the survival of art and the artist. The absolutist critic of either camp must therefore be neutralized, refuted, given no quarter, especially if he appeals to history for a verdict on the power of revolution to produce art. He is wrong and had better leave the past alone, not to mention the present and its nascent art.

As for the future, what has happened twice before need not of course happen a third time. But it seems likely that to change the relation between revolution and culture would require a different sort of political leader, a different sort of artist and of humanity—which is impossible, because no matter what its future hopes about changing the world may be, a revolution always starts in the present, with humanity as it is in the present.

The great theorists of revolution, Marx, Engels, and Lenin, were highly cultivated men and they confirm this view.[12] Their testimony is abundant though scattered, but it all points the same way. Writing to a friend who had published a poetical work of strong revolutionary tendency, Engels said:—

> This is now done, it lies behind you and you have no need of repeating it in the present form. I am by no means an opponent of tendentious poetry as such. The father of tragedy, Aeschylus, and the father of comedy, Aristophanes, were both strongly tendentious poets,* Dante and Cervantes no less so. . . . But I think the tendency must spring out of the situation and action themselves, without being expressly pointed out, and the poet is under no necessity of putting into the reader's hand the historically future solution of the social conflict he depicts.

Marx, who in the *Communist Manifesto* complained of artists being the paid wage earners of the capitalist class, had no great desire to see them become the paid wage earners of any other group, In talking about art,

* But Aristophanes, for one, took the liberty of writing a play which criticized at its height a war that his homeland, Athens, was waging. Personal insults seasoned this piece of political defeatism which no modern state, democratic or not, would have the courage to tolerate.

he always kept in mind the gap that separates, though it does not divide, the social and economic system from the ultimate aspect and value of art. Greek art, for example, was to him a model of simplicity and strength, even though he was the first to recognize that it was rooted in slavery and exploitation.

Lenin, throughout his entire career as theorist and maker of revolutions, maintained that "proletarian culture is not something that jumps up from nobody knows where. It is not a thought-up scheme of some people who call themselves specialists in proletarian culture. That is all pure nonsense. . . . Proletarian culture must come forth as a natural development. . . . Every artist, everybody who wishes to, can claim the right to create freely according to his ideal." When someone proposed in the Council of People's Commissars to close the Great Theatre because it seemed a needless expense to produce bourgeois works in a year of scarcity, Lenin replied: "It seems to me that Comrade Galkin has a somewhat naïve idea of the rôle and significance of theatres. A theatre is necessary not so much for propaganda as to rest hard workers after their daily toil. And it is still early to file away in the archives our heritage from bourgeois art."

With backing from such high authorities, it is not unfair to conclude that the dangers involved in the system of revolution applied to art are dangers not only to art and to democratic freedom but to revolution itself. The confusion between the uses of art and those of a "weapon," the failure to see that the one re-creates reality with all its conflicts while the other limits thought for the sake of hurried action, leads to the production not of art but of rubbish. It makes the revolution sterile and ridiculous in the eyes of posterity to the very extent that the art-thirsty revolutionists pull and tug at culture's skirts. The greatest art can without doubt reflect the *politics* of an era—witness Aristophanes and Dante—but it cannot embody the *policies* of a given week. Urgency of the kind that revolutionary leaders plead justifies many things; it may be reasonable to ask a pamphleteer or an orator to square his inspiration with the chosen tactics, but it is absurd to ask the musician and the chemist to do so. It was Napoleon in his dictatorial phase who wrote to his Commissioner of Police asking him why there was no flourishing literature in the Empire and please to see to it that there was.

In criticism, the judgment of works of art by inquiry into their social origins leads to the distortion of all past art. Lenin protested against this in behalf of Tolstoy's works, knowing that this "filing away of the bourgeois heritage" can only mean a net loss of culture. Retaining that heritage signifies no compromise but a recognition that art is not literal. If the heroine of a novel to which credence was given in the earnest Thirties could have forgotten that Mozart wore a wig and played to royalty, she would not have wanted to "throw open the windows" when Mozart was being played. If the Marxist scholars of that time had shrugged off the false necessity of converting the dead to Marxism, they would not have written that Shakespeare's "revolutionary criticism has never been wholly accepted by the bourgeoisie"; nor would they have found in Malvolio, Shylock, and Iago "representatives of the English middle class which Shakespeare scathingly denounces."[13] If Shakespeare denounces anything in Malvolio it is the Puritan, the system maker, the stiff revolutionist, for whom there are no more cakes and ale because he is virtuous and dedicated.

It is a dangerous weakness to be forever searching into the works of dead authors for literal traces of modern ideas. It is a messianic view of literature which commits anachronism for the sake of assured prophecy. It acts powerfully on young or untrained minds seeking to educate themselves, and only serves to cut them off from the enjoyment of certain authors. Unfortunately, putting these in quarantine for their political sins, real or imaginary, is to punish ourselves far more than them.

In art that is being made, any flattery and glorification of the proletarian is a contradiction both in cultural and in revolutionary thinking. The very notion of the classless state means that the proletarian will be forgotten as a monstrous growth which the revolution was specially designed to abolish. Long before that time the proletarian hero embalmed in a work of art will grow as tedious as the French revolutionary patriot and his virtue, and will fail to fulfill Lenin's requirement of resting hard workers after their toil.

Those who seek to justify a revolutionary movement by pointing to its supposed artistic merits are misusing art for its "conspicuous consumption" value. The procedure is a piece of snobbery. Any revolution that can improve the lot of mankind will be gratefully remembered by posterity even though it has not left us a single great lyric; and on the other hand, no amount of lyrics with or without doctrine will compensate mankind for the evil of fear and oppression under whatever flag or philosophy it may parade.

With dictators killing or silencing gifted men for the sake of a uniform culture, and well-meaning theorists of revolution warping art to a preconceived pattern, it is not hard to see why the maintenance of cultural democracy is more necessary than ever. Social-minded thought and art we must have, for there is no other kind. But we shall soon have no art or thought whatever if we continue to act on the notion that culture is to be tested by a rigidly prescribed subject matter and political point of view.

If we brush aside the suspicion that the criterion of revolution is often used among us to carry on a petty artists' war in the name of something big, we are left with an important general conclusion: all totalitarians take it for granted that art bears some relation to society, but they do not believe it strongly enough to let that relation take care of itself. They decide what it shall be and enforce it with threats to life and limb. Either they do not trust their own theory to work itself out, or they do not trust their own society to produce the kind of art they want. In either case they betray their very feeble understanding of artistic psychology, of economic causation, and of the way in which art is indeed a criticism of life.

It would be idle to pretend that the upholders of democracy, here or abroad, are limpid pools of wisdom on these same subjects. For one thing, few people care enough about art to study and control their own ideas and feelings about it. For another, we have got accustomed to a natural flow of art from men whom we neglect during their lifetime and canonize when dead. We are consumers indifferent to our source of supply. A few great critics have taught us to repeat tags about social art and criticism of life, native tradition and democratic culture, but without moving us to look into the how and why. We are therefore in the awkward position of being suddenly assaulted by opponents of our state and society on a ground we have seldom if ever surveyed. We have a vague preference for *laisser faire* in artistic matters, but we do not really know whom to let alone and what we shall receive in exchange for the privilege. I have tried to point the "lesson of art," which is that art mirrors diversity and refutes absolutism. I must now show how far a democracy can rely on a natural supply of art, what its duties are in the matter of "accepting" it, and what fads, fallacies, and other dangers perpetually threaten it in our midst, from the schoolroom where literature is made into poison, all the way to the concert hall where Bach is snobbishly endured as a maker of absolute music and absolute boredom.

5 *The Arts, the Snobs,*
and the Democrat

IF a democratic society is left to is own devices, what kind
of art can it expect? Henry Adams, almost fifty years ago,
was already concerned over the frittering away of cultural
energy that might result from free democracy.[1] His assumption was that in the past, notably in the Middle
Ages, there was an imposed standard to give coherence to
individual effort, a central authority to pay for great
works of art, and a consequent richness of production.
Moreover, having an absolute standard, the artist could
warn, instruct, and glorify what was socially sound. He
could criticize life and mould it to a comon morality.

This is an historical appeal which must be met at the
outset with two denials. The absolute unity of the medieval scene is imaginary rather than real, and the criticism-
of-life theory is recent. It is in fact contemporary with democracy as we know it. If we pick up the critical works of
Aristotle, Pope, or Lessing, we are at once struck by the
fact that they were hardly concerned about the poet's rap-
port with his environment. He was said to write well or
ill according as he possessed skill and inventiveness, judgment and power. Those were the variables, while Nature
was One. The spirit or breath that made the artistic mill
go round was supposed to originate in the bosoms of nine
barefoot ladies, as old as the hills they trod, and who no
longer bothered to suit their attire to changes in fashion.

Since about 1800, owing chiefly to the historical-minded Romanticists, criticism has changed. Nature means a particular clime and time. Art is a particular, personal gift. We expect individual forms from individual talents. We clamor for an Amercan literature, native music, and circumstantial landscapes. We put the artist on the spot and expect him to stay there. The products of art must smell of the soil, or at least of the asphalt of a particular city. Woe to the poet whose free verse is too free of vital statistics, or to the novelist who does not "formulate" properly! We demand, but how do we provide?

The usual reply is that great art flourishes whenever the civilization as a whole is great and wherever there is a people with high artistic ideals. The mind leaps back to the Greeks (a people entirely composed of artists), then to the age that built the cathedrals (an age entirely peopled by mystics)—and stops there. The argument runs in a circle: a civilization is great because of its art and conversely.

The commonplaces about the Greeks and the cathedrals furnish but one useful clue to the relation between art and society. They suggest that art has to be paid for, if only to keep the artists alive. Now people will pay for something only if they think it worth having; if they can, as the phrase goes, appreciate it. Art can flourish only in a civilization that enjoys a little superfluity of goods and whose population has some little respect for art. So far the reasoning is familiar enough. When it is applied to our own society it seems to break down. We certainly possess as large a material surplus as any previous civilization, and we have high ideals enshrined in familiar platitudes. But ask any social-minded critic what the present relation of the artist to society is and he answers: Divorce. The artist is divorced from society. Society does not support him adequately; his social status is uncertain, and his productions are either soliloquies or else syntheses of the world

66

spirit that the world spirit refuses to recognize. We blame democracy or capitalism or the shortage of genius, but we do not deem ourselves as culturally well off as the Greeks of Pericles's time or the medieval inhabitants of Chartres.

Generalities about a "whole people" are likely to be wrong, and if we take a look at the Greeks of Pericles's time we are sure of it. The Greeks, to begin with, were only the Athenians with a sprinkling of resident foreigners; they were a cityful not of esthetes but of politicians, businessmen, idlers, and slaves. The passion for the arts was limited to a few contemplative souls, the same who cultivated philosophy, science, and the making of utopias. We always quote Pericles's boast about cultivating art without effeminacy, but we conveniently forget that he also said the deeds of the Greek soldiers were the best proof of Athens' greatness, and that "far from needing a Homer for our panegyrist, or other of his craft whose verses might charm for the moment . . . we have forced every sea and land to be the highway of our daring, and everywhere, whether for evil or for good, have left imperishable monuments behind us."

The Greeks who did not need Homer are of course the same Greeks who built the Acropolis, carved the frieze of the Parthenon, and wrote immortal books; but they are the "same" only in the usual sense in which artists and their society are identified. Artists and philosophers then as now met with disapproval or encouragement, were rewarded, exiled, or put to death according to the usual chances of life. They left artistic monuments behind them because they individually struck a balance of conditions in their favor, not because Greek society as a whole was purposely designed to foster art. Except for the artists themselves, art was but an adjunct to religion and civic pride.[2]

The Romans similarly valued works of art; a few for the sake of art itself and the rest for the sake of conspicuous consumption. After the disintegration of Rome, the Christian faith used art largely as propaganda and it was only after the lapse of a few centuries that this faith became so taken for granted as to permit free expression for the artist. He could then work with naïveté or sophistication and remain free on the doctrinal side, sure of his audience and supported financially by the church. This financing, however, was anything but the spontaneous offering of a "whole people" that some modern collectivists like to dwell on. Like the Pyramids, the cathedrals were put up with the aid of forced labor and forced contributions, which does not, of course, exclude true religious emotion or civic pride.

The Western tradition about art seems fairly uniform: art is tolerated and financed as an aid to patriotism and religion, but even then only when the religion is so well established and the patriotism so circumscribed that they seem, not the fruits of indoctrination, but rather an obvious truth and a universal feeling. Athenian patriotism was of that kind, for the city was the only source of protection for the individual, and was also an object of religious worship. On a broader intellectual and geographical basis, the church of the Middle Ages produced the stained glass and architecture of the cathedrals and the illuminations of the monastery, but church and monastery were maintained as public and private expense for other, more immediate reasons than the pure love of art.

2

The modern period has seen a rapid succession of methods for financing art and artists. The Italian despots and Popes were patrons, like the kings of France and England, partly for show and partly from genuine love of art. Richelieu and Colbert's system of pensions brought with it a kind of journalistic obligation. They were the first to pay regularly for propaganda. Music was supported in the same practical way. It was a commodity for use with meals, at weddings, and so forth.

In literature, the successful change from patronage to public subscription came in the eighteenth century, traditionally with Pope's translation of Homer, which netted him a fortune before its completion. Since then, with some exceptional throwbacks to the system of state sinecures, literature has depended in one form or another upon public favor, while the more expensive arts of architecture, painting, drama, and music have been paid for partly by the public, partly by the state.

It is within the most recent period, say the last seventy-five years, that there has been increasing talk of the divorce between the artist and society. National patriotism and the Protestant sects have neither of them been productive in the same sense as ancient patriotism and medieval religion. These older emotions have been replaced by others equally strong but not nearly so unanimous within the given society. It is this unanimity that totalitarians of all kinds are seeking to restore and it is the diversity that democracy supposedly values, though it neglects to pay for it.

The result is that unless his genius permits him to have a wide appeal, the modern artist must live on some form of charity. A great painter like Daumier cannot sell his pictures and dies in a house given him by a friend. A great architect like Louis Sullivan dies with plans for buildings never built because fame was too slow in coming. Or a great poet like Walt Whitman ends his days in obscurity and misery as if his life had been idle and profligate.

At the same time, "going concerns" like orchestral societies, museums, and opera houses must continually beg from their patrons and trustees; they almagamate or stop activities for lack of funds.[3] Literature somehow pays its

Of Human Freedom

own way, although poetry and works of a philosophical
cast are generally "carried" by cultured publishers out of
the proceeds of best sellers. Scholarship that lacks visible
social utility is almost exclusively supported by foundations and universities, that is, lives on charity. There is
a gap between what we pretend to want as a civilization
and what we are willing to pay for as a people.

The spread of literacy has added confusion to natural
avarice. A vastly increased public now demands and gets
a vast amount of literature, painting, and music. But this
culture is designed for an audience whose tastes seldom
stray from the comfortable love story, the pretty picture,
or the catchy tune.* Banality, a simple moral, and a soothing effect constitute for that public the artistic experience; and the same education which has created the public has enabled a great many industrious workers to supply
the demand.

Discussions about art are consequently vitiated by a
confusion between art of this easy-going kind, intended
for daily consumption, and art of a different kind, designed for connoisseurs.⁴ Of the former kind our society
probably has more, and pays better for it in the shape of
movies, novels, and magazines, than any previous civilization. And contrary to current belief, the making of "consumer" art is by no means easy and by no means repre-
hensible. Indignation is as out of place in speaking of
jazz or a Sousa march as it is in front of a dish of boiled
potatoes; and the refusal to call the march music is as
critically unsound as to refuse to call the potatoes food.

The distinction between the two types of art is a difference of density rather than of species. In the same number
of bars of Beethoven and of Sousa, there is, in Beethoven,
more of the essence of music, giving a thicker, more in-
tense effect likely to alienate the unfamiliar listener by

* There are supposed to be 15,000 copyrighted songs beginning "I
love you." The meaning of the word "copyright" acquires from such
statistics an ambiguous if not an ironic sense.

70

"boring him, just as the palate accustomed to that richer food is bored by the thinness of the popular tune.* The feeling that this is not the only difference is due to the fact that as an art grows more and more complex and dense, the number of relations among simple elements increases until those relations look like extraordinarily refined experiences denied to the common herd. Yet there is no real barrier to be leaped over by an effort of genius between understanding a "vulgar" dance tune and a Beethoven symphony.

To have a fitting art, therefore, democracy must steer clear of three fallacious absolutes: One, Tolstoy's demand that art should appeal to the simplest minds as well as the most cultivated. Two, the belief that there is a socially approved list of books, pictures, and symphonies called The Best—an island for the elect in a Sargasso sea of vulgarity. Three, the utopian's desire that everyone become an enthusiastic enjoyer of the arts. At one point these three absolutes converge: the habit of drawing moral distinctions between good and bad, high and low, in art, which hinders everybody from finding his own proper diet. Democratic art *can* mean the same art for everybody, but it must mean also *equivalent* art for different tastes. A deplorable yearning for sameness still seems to haunt the proponents of the good life, although they never explain why everybody should go to the opera rather than to a chess tournament. Nor has it ever been made clear why makers of utopias invariably promise us a leisure full of "pop" concerts and first editions. Why not mathematical congresses and horse races?

As it is we suffer (in both senses) far too much social

---

* This density spoken of here should not be construed in a material sense as meaning more *notes* to the bar or more instruments playing them, but a greater condensation of experience or significance in the ordinary means employed—melody, rhythm, harmony, and so forth. The magic involved defies analysis, as one feels on realizing the effect produced by a common chord or other simple device in the hands of a great artist.

71

snobbery about art. No predestination of birth or brains selects those for whom the arts are meaningful, and if anything can and ought to be open to free choice, it is the realm of art. Presumably the readers of pulp magazines choose the one they like—detective or erotic—but in the so-called upper reaches of culture many who ought to know better sit through concerts that bore them, feel ashamed of the things they truly enjoy, and think that the pain of tramping through museums is credit to their account in the spiritual bank. Too many artists likewise are warped or thrown into false competition by the snobbery of critics and patrons who would honestly prefer pushpin to poetry, and who pretend at the same time that nothing is good enough for them.

This misguided reverence for the spiritual value of art, this pseudo-democratic desire to give the best of it to everybody, is touching but chimerical. The language of art is a special language, the understanding of which is not limited to any class, race, or nation, and which is completely unteachable by the usual methods. This is obvious enough from the forced feeding of Shakespeare and Scott in the schools. As Hazlitt pointed out long ago, there is no primer to Parnassus. The appreciation of art does not coincide with intelligence, nor even with the abilities of the art dealer or musical performer. What it correlates with no one knows, for a *Varieties of Artistic Experience* has not yet been written.

The fact remains that art is something for the few,[5] and who those few are is unpredictable. They are not superior for being the few, and no proof exists that they are happier. The many, including representatives of the rich, the well-born, and the able, are made acutely unhappy by repeated attempts to kindle art in their soul under forced draft; while the minority is too often badgered by the snobs striving to impose their fashionable favorite on everybody else. Either form of compulsion leaves the great majority indifferent or hostile to art. If this is so, Philistinism had better be accepted as inevitable rather than fought by the undemocratic methods now in use. Its chief danger is not that it interferes with a businesslike financing of art, but rather that it tempts the genuine artist or connoisseur to join a crusade which neither history nor true democracy justifies.

3

And yet, it may be objected, our predecessors in Philistinism left a "characteristic art" to posterity. Whether the profiteers of the Peloponnesian War liked it or not, there stood the Parthenon and there it stands now. How can we be sure that without fascist or revolutionist or snobbish absolutes, a free democracy will endow posterity with forms equally impressive, and expressive too of our feelings and capacities? The question, as we have seen, cannot be resolved out of hand by saying, "Let there be a dictator who is also a great critic," or "Let us set up a board to reward the worthy artist." These devices always rely on political means and are based on political ideas, the mischief of which is that being applied from without they give to art a uniformly flat appearance the very reverse of expressiveness.

A more logical point of attack is the interested customers themselves—the people who want art more than entertainment or luxury.[6] They are few, but they can utilize the wants of the greater number who use art for other purposes than contemplation: those who want, and are willing to pay for, skyscrapers, private houses, packaged goods, decorated walls in public buildings, open-air statuary, tombstones, national pageants, and patriotic poetry. With all these habitual (if not normal) desires functioning and fulfilled, we have a chance to make a good showing in history. They correspond to the patriotic and religious motives of earlier civilizations. The only danger is that these magnificent opportunities will be wasted by repeated concessions to the popular liking for a tame, undisturbing sort of art as nearly like pushpin as possible.

That popular liking is in fact seldom consulted, and what it objects to is not art itself but novelty, which offends visual and other habits. If the offending object outstays the old habit, a new habit will form. That is how national styles change. The responsibility for great and expressive art therefore falls on the so-called connoisseurs and arbiters of art—the critics, curators, teachers, and historians—who are in positions of authority, who shape the tastes and make the decisions, and who either yield to the fear of popular outcry or brave it in the knowledge that it will die and the work of art remain.

Critical lag or backwardness is thus harmless in the Philistines and fatal among the elite. It is inexcusable in the few who actually have it in their power to choose between the new creation and the hackneyed copy. The ability to make that choice depends on being a connoisseur not only of past, but of living contemporary art. The whole matter of divorcing or remarrying the artist and society comes down to this: If it is possible for a relatively small group of fanciers to "accept" Cézanne and Van Gogh in 1930, there seems to be no reason in the conformation of the human mind why these artists should not have been accepted thirty years before. Nor is there any reason in economics why a canvas by Daumier which could not have been given away in 1875 should now fetch half a million. We imagine that we need time; the fact that critics and public "come around" and are willing at last to like what has been shown them for fifty years when something still newer is brought forth has led to a belief in a dignified critical progress following the artistic evolution at a respectful distance. It is nothing of the kind: it is fatigue.

74

This lesson of art history is never learned, we never catch up with contemporary art, because we are a quarter of a century behindhand with a pile of past art to absorb, a fact which we express with unconscious smugness by saying of the great artist that he was "ahead of his time." The artist, if he is creative at all, is with his time, even when he works against it. He is organizing (pro or con) the perceptions that he acquires from the process of living and not from the contemplation of past art. The public, however, is apparently receptive only to art that looks, not like organized life, but like other art. And the fault— since there is no personal conspiracy or malignity in this vicious circle—lies in our methods of criticism and education.

Complaints against critics are as old as art itself. Swift compared the fraternity to two other ancient and disreputable professions because, like them, critics never change their character or their trade. Many people, feeling the inadequacy of critics, make a point of disregarding them all, together with their academic counterparts, the historians of art. Yet rightly understood, criticism is the quickest way to discover the relation that obtains between an age and its artists, and once we grasp that relation there is a chance that we can understand and "accept" living art without the usual fits and tantrums· of denunciation. What we need is not a knowledge of what art is good, but a knowledge of what good art does. The two things are quite different, though conservative objection to new art always confuses the two. Even the word "connoisseur," which I have been using for want of a better, is misleading. It suggests "the best that has been said and thought in the world," than which there is, by now, no more prissy, inartistic, anti-cultural principle.

But how can the baneful tradition be overcome? Let anyone interested in an artist or work of art turn to the available criticism on the subject, reading not one book but five or six indiscriminately, and the trick is done: the discovery is made that upon the oldest and best-known works of art there is no fundamental agreement. There is no consensus of opinion but a *dis*sensus; no such thing as the judgment of Posterity, but a chaos of contradictory views.[7] The Past, culturally speaking, is not a fixed but a changing thing, different with every new generation. Criticism is not the field of Armageddon, where one battles for the Lord, but Dover Beach, where ignorant armies clash by night.

Art lives in its own day as well as later by virtue of its appeal to some, and not to all, of the connoisseurs of art. There may be an unconscious logrolling among them to accept one another's favorites, but the conflict is real; it is both dishonest and dangerous to gloss it over. To throw out the testimony of a competent critic when he registers his dislike of a great name, say Milton or Brahms, is to treat both art and the critic politically instead of culturally. The chances are that he is an honest observer of his own feelings and of the particular work of art. His refusal to admire is due to a personal limitation, of course, but such a limitation is true of every individual. And the failure is a more universal truth about culture than is the supposedly universal appeal of any great artist.

We speak confidently of world poets; we affirm the international appeal of music; we term classics those works which, we like to think, everyone would agree to regard as first-rate. These generalizations are figments of our conceit, repeated by each little coterie or national group in its own circle. These cliques are like the village dairy that advertises, "Cream sent to all parts of the world." Go from clique to clique and you will awaken to the differences that exist about the merits of the best-established names. Travel from country to country and the elite of each will give you a very different list of world poets; and as for music and painting, no two "lovers" of either art will consent to admit the same dozen names to their private Pantheon.

The motives for humility are not exhausted yet. For one thing, in speaking of universal art we almost always forget the civilizations of China, India, and Japan, comprising far more than half the population of the world, and for whom the "world fame" of a Beethoven or a Shakespeare is a very dim effulgence indeed. For another, even in our restricted circles, the accident of agreement upon certain authors does not mean anything like agreement about their qualities, their best works, or their significance in the history of art. At the risk of tediousness it must be repeated that this diversity does not obtain concerning only recent or second-rate artists, or about inherently controversial figures like Michelangelo, Spinoza, or Berlioz; it obtains about the supposedly solid and accepted ones like Milton, Dante, and Beethoven. The supposed "consensus" is merely a convention which prohibits the voicing of doubts but does not abolish their existence. It is the fashion now to pay lip service to Shakespeare and Bach and Dante, but it has not always been so. And even to-day the number of times that a sincere communion takes place between the works of these artists and the minds of their admirers is, comparatively small.

When, therefore, an honorable citizen of the republic of letters tells us that such or such a Titan is overrated, or empty, or boring, the probability is that he has read him and made the discovery, while we merely repeat old tags of perfunctory admiration. We must in any case listen to his reasons, agree or disagree, but ever resist the temptation of throwing his vote into the wastebasket in order that our candidate may be unanimously elected. Once we make up our minds to accept this democratic diversity in criticism we can enjoy art with decency. Instead of hoping that some day the entire globe will worship at our shrines, or pretending all the while that it does, we discover that varied artistic experiences can be equally valid; we discover that a great work of art is not an absolute good in itself, but a means whereby individual experience is organized and extended; we see that it is our culture and our personal history that push us to Bach and to Dante, as well as an inherent, though not inescapable, good in them that pulls us. The medium of communication is art, but the medium of comprehension is life. As life wears a different aspect for each individual, the language of the artist is bound to carry diverse meanings to each beholder, and sometimes no meaning at all. The diversity of meanings does not cancel them out, nor is there some secret formula of decipherment, differing for each artist, that must be painfully inculcated in the young lest they be eternally damned.

Considered in this light, works of art, instead of stringing themselves along an evolutionary line according to technique, regroup themselves within their historical period. They reveal to the observer what it is that the artists do in paint, words, or sound with the sensations of their time. That is the true relation between art and society which dictators, critics, and prophets are fumbling for. If it could be grasped by any generation of teachers and critics, they would be enabled to leap over the cultural lag of twenty-five years and understand their own artists; they could select with less fear of being duped, and instead of seeing chaos or believing in decadence; they would find a few common tendencies under the surface variety of style, subject matter, and message.

This hope of a critically alert culture may be visionary, but it is at any rate worth pursuing. All the other methods seem to have failed, though we refuse to acknowledge the failure. We blame the artist, the government, the economic system—anybody and anything but ourselves—complaining century after century of "sterility" and "de-

cadence" in arts and artists which our posterity finds alive
and kicking.

4

I have said that the language of art is not teachable by
an analysis of techniques, nor explained by an application to the ordinary histories of art. What is taught in
schools and printed in textbooks—usually in despair of
anything better—is not so much wrongheaded as over-
schematic and absolute-minded.[8] Literature is scanned
for references to contemporary events; "influences" are
traced, which usually means that similarities are found—
a very different thing; lives of artists are consulted in the
hope of linking the mood of a poem with the domestic
joys and calamities of the author. All these attempts are
illusory so far as "explanation" is concerned. The "factors" sought for may be real and relevant, but they act
in more indirect and complex ways than anyone knows.
Scholarship can lay the foundations but cannot supply
the understanding: we have learned little about music
when we know that Mozart wrote a gay symphony under
conditions of sorrow; we are no closer to Courbet's painting when we find he was affiliated with the Paris Commune.

If not through bare historical pickings, nor through
technical analysis, nor through systematic search for this
and that, how can we get the "feel" for art which is
prerequisite to understanding its individual and social
function? Chiefly through multiplied contacts with art
of all periods and all kinds. Then through a deliberate
discarding of all acquired responses save pleasure. Political partisanship, "improving oneself," or agreeing
with the best people must be overcome within. Only
when art is taken unaffectedly, as a conversation with the
dead or distant, free from ulterior motives and from

pride of knowledge, will the dates, life histories, and technical details find their proper place. Instead of barring the road, they fill out the landscape of art.

Discussing pure poetry or speculating whether Balzac's works have a right to be called novels—I have even heard it maintained that Beethoven's works were not "strictly" music—can only be the pastimes of people for whom art itself is too strong a dose of seriousness and fun, and who prefer logomachy to experience. Such a preference usually ends in a cult for a single artist: everything else becomes too rash, too imperfect, not pure enough for the delicate appetite fed only on the best.

The entire history of art condemns these confining dogmas. Technique, tradition, narrow disdains and dislikes, creeds of the pure and the absolute, national and provincial ideals, are the hobgoblins of the pseudo-cultured. Technique and Tradition have been means to an end, and they will continue to be so with alterations and additions by creative minds. They are strong and real enough to need no coddling and codifying at the hands of people who, while they are the "intelligent posterity" of yesterday, are the "blind contemporaries" of to-day. The only rule of art and the only safe prediction regarding its course is that the unexpected always happens. Its corollary is that no sooner has a critic or an age demonstrated by *a* plus *b* that some artistic purpose or device is impossible than an artist is found somewhere successfully doing it. The utter futility of legislating for art, and the complete uselessness of copying former masterpieces, should be the first tenets of any practical plan of art teaching and art appreciation.

A democracy where the individual can freely choose his cultural sustenance can safely leave to human genius the making of an art adequate to its greatness. The way is perhaps inefficient, but it is less harmful than the deadly efficiency of the political mentors or the state patronage of the older democratic countries.

Even under artistic *laisser faire,* however, there are certain cultural duties. For the masses of the citizens they are negative: hands off. For those more immediately concerned with the arts, they are more strenuous. Granting freedom to the artist means relieving him from the necessity of justifying himself; showing a greater appetite for a variety of styles and individual manners; stifling critical suspiciousness and doctrinaire expectations; and taking what is offered for what it is worth instead of trying to make it fit into the set categories of what is American, or modern, or classical, or proletarian. The desirable pragmatic attitudes toward art may be difficult to instil even in the small group directly interested in culture. But a beginning might be made through our schools where there has long been a distrust of fixity and of the absolute True, Good, and Beautiful. Any small gain in this direction would go far towards lessening the cultural pressure on the whole nation and thus permit it to foster (and finance) more freely its own art in its own day, for its own pleasure and the incidental edification of posterity.

6 *"Reality"*—*Loud Cheers*

THE last three chapters have taken it for granted that art matters. It is a notion borrowed from the dictators, the critics, and the political thinkers in our midst. The democrat, too, is convinced that we must display a cultural front, for we have come to think of nations as our grandmothers thought of young ladies—none can be called accomplished unless there is a bit of embroidery or water color lying about.

But cutting across this modern sentiment there is an equally widespread and contradictory feeling that all art is "escape," that intelligence is a disease, and that the whole concern with culture is "unrealistic." Some people, it seems, have a secure hold on reality while the rest flounder about in illusion. For the latter we have a word: neurotic. Every attitude we fear, every occupation we condemn, is neurotic. Hitler was neurotic and so was Walt Whitman. But some artists and statesmen are even worse: they are psychotic. Van Gogh was insane and so was President Roosevelt. It is an ascending scale of damnation.

For those useful words neurotic and psychotic we are indebted to the psychiatrists, and as they are increasingly tempted to guide us through the emotional tangles of our time, we must, if only in self-defense, hear and assess their counsels. But an even more pressing task is to try to understand why intelligence and culture are considered unreal, while bombs, clever lies, and common lusts constitute the only reality. In dealing with these choices about what is "really real" we are of course dealing with popularized science and psychology—a mixture of Eddington and Jeans talking of atoms with Freud exploring the human soul. Leaving the nature of science aside for the moment, let us see what the general theory of psychoanalysis says about culture and reality. For it is plain that in talking glibly of neurosis, reality, and sex, or of the struggle between instinct and intellect, the common man has forgotten that these are technical terms. We know that when he says "neurotic" he is merely calling names, but what is his status when he appeals to reality and condemns something or somebody as unrealistic and escapist?

Nobody likes to be told that he is "imagining things," so the word "reality" has become a term of praise, as Eddington himself aptly pointed out by quoting the close of a political speech: ". . . Reality! (Loud cheers)."[1] But when one asks for a convenient test of what is real and what is not, the cheering tends to subside. Dr. Karen Horney,[2] the psychoanalyst, gives us an essential clue when she says that to diagnose a neurotic requires a knowledge of the culture in which he lives. The culture or society makes the reality with which he is at odds; therefore the Indian boy who sees visions is "normal" and at one with his culture, whereas the American boy who sees them is "abnormal" and alone in his hallucination. Reality is a kind of convention. So put, the definition may be hard to accept, yet we act upon it in daily life, and the testimony of history and anthropology is behind it. Science and philosophy point in the same direction. If the entire human race were color-blind, the "real" world would be colorless. That being so, "reality" is colorless for color-blind people, just as it is soundless for us when our dog hears a whistle inaudible to us.

Since, however, not all agree about colors, mankind compares the varying reports of its senses and accepts the testimony of the majority, supplemented by that of the inquiring—the philosophers and men of science. This investigation scarcely changes the nature of individual reality. For each of us reality is what we perceive. Even when we grant that others perceive things that pass us by, those things seem faint and dim, and we are more aware of the fact that others differ from us than of the things differed about. This fact of consciousness explains why there is no ultimate agreement about life and why in art and thought we respond to certain authors and not to others. A poem, a philosophy, may contain heavenly music and divine wisdom, but it is not, as we say, "for us."

It follows that no work of art, no occupation, no attitude, denotes by itself an escape from reality. Unless we are escapists every time we turn our attention from one thing to another, the charge of escapism has no meaning. What turns our attention here or there is our desire, our instinct—Sex, if we take the word in the inclusive sense Freud means to give it. Our desires are always real, but we are moved by so many that we must choose. At this point fitness of choice (which is intelligence) or habit (which is past choice) leads to acts which either satisfy or frustrate desire. What leads to success we call "realistic," success being definable in many ways, from the commonplace usage of business to the subtle attribution of "success" to perfect art.

Since consequences come home most vividly through the thwarting of desire, men tend to think that what is most unpleasant is most real, whence the idea that art, being pleasant, must be *un*real. The reasoning is false, yet one feels that those who take art tragically or who grow despondent over the evils of the world are equally morbid, abnormal, out of gear with "reality." What determines reality and normality (two aspects of one elusive thing) is then the democratic consensus regarding what is in the main useful or desirable for society. To be sure, the tests of utility and pleasure tend to become habitual rather than accurate. No one thinks planting geraniums is odd, because it is done every day. But the man who digs for treasure in his back garden is looked upon as a trifle cracked. As a matter of fact, the soil of the garden may be unfit for geraniums, in which case it is folly to plant them, and the previous owner may have buried his hoard there, in which case it is eminently sane to look for it. The utmost sanity or "realism" consists only in this—judging each case right and acting appropriately.

In a complex world this program is not practicable. We must go by signs, preconceived ideas, prejudices and superstitions. It is in part this necessity that makes the neurotic. The neurotic is known by his rigidity.[3] He does things not because they are appropriate, but because he must do something and can only conceive or carry out the inappropriate. His making the same mistake again and again is the expression of his rigidity.

Since in the welter of modern life we cannot always act appropriately, we are all neurotics to a greater or lesser extent. But some achieve in a limited realm a high degree of appropriateness. The artist is one of these successful men, masters of reality: he may act neurotically to his landlady, but he reaches the acme of sanity in paint or words. The statesman is another; the scientist is a third. They are all successful to the exact extent that they are not neurotic.

The measure of success in this special sense is naturally impossible to state, and often enough society's neglect of a given effort negates its reality. A hundred years ago, many cultivated people trained in music found the later works of Beethoven "insane"—that is, not in keeping with the prevailing notions of what music should be. To-day we laugh at these people, accept Beethoven, and call insane some more recent musician. But this is no guarantee that we shall revise our notions about *him*.

What the artist or scientist does is to add to our notions of reality if he can. He creates it out of his peculiar desires and perceptions. The artist seizes upon a feeling or a likeness we have passed over without giving it a name, points to an experience we have overlooked, and by fitting it memorably into a scheme of things we already know, compels us to take in what he has embodied. At that point we say we give him recognition, whereas what we actually recognize is a fresh aspect of reality. Artists are thus aptly called creators, not because they handle material stuff, but because they add a piece to the body of existing, communicable, social reality.

2

The political application is simple: if reality is at once individual, like perception, and social, like "normality," then free democracy, with its diversity and flexibility, clearly parallels the human mind functioning at its best. By the use of will and intelligence, social order, like artistic order, is constantly being made and won; it cannot be achieved once for all and stay put. Culture is a common heritage which can be added to or changed, but not against our will. For example, the fact that an alien governmental philosophy has conquered another five hundred square miles somewhere on the planet does not by itself damage our own beliefs. Nothing compels us to imitate it and let it rule over our minds and bodies. If we resist with our minds, our bodies have a chance to be free. Free democracy is a reality insofar as we sustain it.

Only in one respect—and I admit its importance—are we helpless and "conditioned": any government, any culture, any organized social life, clamps down the absolutes of custom and convention upon us, and succeeds in making millions of neurotics ready for more absolutes. Fascism, which erects rigidity into an ideal, is neurotic on principle, just as certain lesser bodies—the family, the school, the church—tend to be from habit. We must resist institutional absolutes, but this does not mean that anarchy should be our goal. Anarchy would only land us into the opposite absolute of gang warfare and perpetual fear. The central problem for a nation or for a man is therefore to strike a balance between rule and free choice and to assign each its place. No one is made neurotic by having to drive on the right-hand side of the road; and a thousand such rules may be expedient for economic or social organization. Cultural tyranny is another thing. It manhandles the substance of individual life and cripples social intelligence. Where the barrier to interference is to be put is a matter for endless research; no rule can be given about it that is not absurd or useless. At every moment, we must choose betwen habitual action and thoughtful action, between Dogma and Pragma. The rightness of our choice comes out in the sequel and depends on our imagination, our artistic or political sense —on our intelligence, in short, which seeks a way between the reality of our wishes and the previous realities of the outer world.

Believing this to be a correct description, I cannot wholly agree with Thomas Mann's conclusion about the position of Freud in modern thought. In Mann's view, "Freud unquestionably belongs with those writers of the nineteenth century who . . . stand opposed to rationalism, intellectualism, classicism, in a word to the belief in Mind . . . emphasizing instead the night side of nature, and the soul as the actually life-conditioning and life-giving element. . . . Backwards is the cry; back into the night, the sacred primitive, the romantical, prehistoric mother-womb. That is the language of reaction. But the emphasis is revolutionary."[4]

Later on in his essay, Mann redefines the words "revolution," "romanticism," and "reaction," which enables him to say that psychoanalysis is not politically reactionary, and that mind is not excluded from Freud's "pansexualism." But Mann's first statement about Freud's antagonism to reason has become a commonplace especially for those who have never read Freud and Mann, and its dangerous falsehood must be shown. The familiar way of discrediting reason these days is to appeal to the hard-boiled, "realistic" principle that the instinctive desires of man, on the one hand, and sticks and stones, on the other, form the whole of reality. All theory and intelligence being thus excluded are thereby proved to be a mere froth upon life, a by-product of solid experience having no effect upon it. This dismissal of intellect is called a reaction against the tyranny of rationalism, a fresh start to which has been given the name of activism.

Anything that savors of action nowadays becomes a term of praise, like reality. But the use of rationalism as a term of dispraise makes one suspect a juggling with words. Psychoanalysis rightly interpreted gives us the clue to the confusion: to be rational is to see purposes and choose among them in the light of consequences. The instincts are irrational because their single purpose is to obtain satisfaction regardless of consequences. What the mind does in being rational is to sort out, reconcile, and prefer one activity to another: we cannot, for example, eat and sleep at the same time. To "give up" rationality is therefore as impossible as to give up being a biped. The very giving up (or its advocacy) is itself a rational act, a choice. Contrariwise, irrationality (or desire) enters into every clear thought and is the driving force behind every human act. There is as much irrationality in the writing of poetry as in the breaking of windows. What the "activists" exchange is not the rational life for the life of instinct but one complex rational scheme of life for another.

In the restless parts of western culture where Reason is

said to be rejected, what has taken place is a mere substitution of ideas. Thinking has been represented as a form of paralysis and action made to mean violence. It is argued that thought has never produced anything but doubt, whereas force builds civilization. Under the influence of these tales we forget that although great civilizations have been protected by fighters they were built by people who thought great thoughts—who invented the arch or the alphabet or solved the sides of the right-angle triangle. Strong-arm defense against barbarians is necessary, but where is the parallel to-day? Who are acting like barbarians and destroying the fruits of civilization? Even admitting the presence of an eternal barbarian in our midst and the necessity for checking him, the brawn that does it will in the end prove no substitute for brains. Valuing strength alone is like congratulating the stones of the Parthenon and scorning Phidias. It is again to mistake cause and condition—the fatal mistake of our pseudo-scientific generation.*

For many intellectuals who expected that a good book or leading article would change the face of the world, action may seem the only way to retrieve self-respect. For them, the plunge into war or some other form of movement may well be a personal redemption. But if it is meant to save society, the war or movement must be planned pragmatically and led by thinking minds. The action must fit, or else remain an outlet for neurotic steam. Moreover the aims of the activist intellectual must be those of his war or his party, otherwise he is not engaging in action but going through motions. Action for its own sake is a St. Vitus's dance, a disease and not a cure for the world. And not only fitness of action but scale of aim must be considered. No one can undertake to beat down or channel off the entire world's supply of barbaric instinct and so insure the triumph of civiliza-

* See below, pp. 99, 105, 108, 119–120.

tion. Irrationality is bottled up within every individual body and can only be used and controlled individually.

The great merit of psychoanalysis has been to look the irrational instincts in the face and admit them as legitimate. Their control is not putting down the devil, but utilizing a blind force like fire or falling water. Man is to do to his instincts what he does to nature, harness the power and put it to some use. The head and the heart, the flesh and the spirit, which have been looked upon for centuries as fighting an endless battle, must henceforth be looked upon as a team pulling in the same direction. That is the reason why psychoanalysis as an individual or social cure is not something to be got out of a book but is an experience partaking equally of emotion and intellect. That is also why Freud is not an anarchist or an anti-rational philosopher, and therefore gives no countenance to those who would go "back into the night" and act there like maniacs, on the pretext that their minds had served them ill in the light of open day.

3

We started with the cries of "Neurotic," "Escapist," and "Give us Reality" which fill our ears, and have been led, via psychoanalysis, to consider how our desires, working through something we call mind, manage to get satisfaction from a refractory world. In seeking satisfaction we create pictures of that world, and those that "work" in the broad sense of sating our multitudinous desires—physical, moral, and esthetic—constitute our culture and our reality. Since we individually help make reality and thus approach the order we desire, a democracy of efforts follows necessarily. Desire operating through mind shapes purpose, which branches out in the form of theories, arts, sciences—all pragmatic in nature and true as far as they go, false and dangerous when misapplied or held as absolutes.

It should seem as if this were the end of our quest. We have a working hypothesis: take it or leave it, according to democratic choice. But there is one last stumbling block to be removed: it is in Freud, whom I have so far gratefully followed, and in the mind of many others. I refer to the belief that whereas science gives us a faithful chart of the outside world, art supplies only an agreeable illusion. The error in this distinction does not appear until we try to apply psychoanalytic criticism to culture and to psychoanalysis itself as a psychology of the human mind.

Nothing is more common nowadays than biography or criticism ostensibly based on psychoanalysis. Most of it boils down to the amateurish use of technical terms—hysterical, impotent, neurotic, and the like—to explain the behavior of the great and the products of their minds. But Freud himself has attempted this retrospective judgment and arrived at what he thinks is the "analysis" of a dead artist through the interpretation of the artistic symbols found in his work. The method is the clinical one of discovering the meaning of the patient's symbols and finding their genesis and order. In thus extending his curative technique to art, Freud has overlooked two facts. He fails to see, first, that in psychoanalyzing art he has far less evidence to work with than in two or three years of daily sessions with a patient; and, second, he is led by this scarcity to attach a single meaning to each symbol. He takes the connection for granted and thus destroys the notion of symbols altogether. They become firsthand facts which do not need interpretation in any real sense. All the critic requires is a dictionary of meanings, like people who carry on a courtship in the language of the flowers.[5]

But what has this foreshortening of a method, it may be asked, to do with the culture of democracy? Only this, that in making the meaning of art or ideas correspond inevitably to certain symbols or material facts, we are back in a mindless universe where nothing is created, because everything is prefigured in what went before. We are back where we were with the absolutist minions of Hitler or Stalin who knew at a glance what color or dance movement is inherently bourgeois or Aryan. We are back with the strict materialists and mechanists, whose rigid system compels them to construct an endless-chain universe, a kind of coat of mail into which every individual is born and from which there is no outlet.

Freud's error about art—which he calls a "beneficent illusion"—is in direct contradiction to the rest of his method and of his genius. Nor is the reason hard to find. He wishes above all things to have his work recognized as science. Having been cruelly mistreated by fellow scientists in his early career, he wishes recognition to come from the same quarter where he was first condemned. And having grown up in an age when science implied a machine-like materialism, he has adopted that philosophy as indispensable. The irony of it is that the physical sciences are more and more abandoning mechanism in favor of a more accurate pragmatism which Freud attacks as "anarchy." He says: "According to this anarchistic doctrine there is no such thing as truth, no assured knowledge of the external world. What we give out as scientific truth is only the product of our own needs and desires as they are formulated under varying external conditions; that is to say, it is illusion once more. Ultimately, we find only what we need to find and see only what we desire to see. We can do nothing else. And since the criterion of truth—correspondence with the external world—disappears, it is absolutely immaterial what views we accept."[6]

It is hard to believe that this is Freud speaking and putting into the mouths of his fancied opponents a mixture of folly and of his own procedure. How can he, or any analyst, ask us to believe that what psychoanalysis deals with—the Subconscious, the Ego, the Super-ego—

are ready-made objects in the external world? The truth is that they are features of a conceptual scheme, inventions of a great mind for dealing with effects observed in practice. Their ability to work—to work cures, that is— is the best measure of their "truth." If correspondence with the external world were the only test, they would have to be declared untrue, for no one can extract the super-ego from the body and pickle it in alcohol to convince skeptical materialists.

The pragmatic ways of psychoanalysis are also evident in Freud's own modifications of his original ideas. Like the atom or the ether, Freud's definitions have been changed for the sole purpose of more closely fitting the facts, which is thoroughly scientific conduct. But if that is so, then why pretend that anybody thinks "it is absolutely immaterial what views we accept"? What view we accept determines the measure of our success, in art, in science, in politics; the gaining of happiness through knowledge waits upon the appearance of great views such as Galileo's or Kepler's or Freud's.

The lesser views by which we organize our own chaos are no less pragmatic, no less works of art. Some people can live only by thinking that they are the Empress Josephine. They do not obtain much satisfaction, and may actually run into dangers, hence we lock them up. Other people—Prime Ministers for example—imagine that they are running the country, but it is a harmless idea which many conspire to support, so we do not lock them up. To a third party, say an historian, the two cases may look like equally bad thinking,* bad art, yet the method in both is perfectly sound. Josephine and the "real" Prime Minister and his constituents have all made or borrowed an order that fits to the best of their ability

* That is what Brougham thought when he said, "As for Lord Liverpool, he is no more Prime Minister than I am," and went on to show that the Lord Chancellor, Eldon, really ruled England. See Walter Bagehot, *Literary Studies.*

what they see and feel. If all lives were not fashioned so, in the pragmatic faith that they are real and useful, life itself would stop. The artist, the traffic policeman, the certified public accountant, would all suddenly discover that their activities are useless and fantastic, that only the direct gratification of instincts is real, and that society is a dream from which we only wake to die.

In this last case, and only in such a case, is the revolt against intellect, the belief that art is illusion and that we are puppets blown hither and yon, pardonable. All other views implicitly or explicitly affirm the contrary: the most convinced materialist and "realitarian" still tries to persuade us by arguments. He seeks to reach our minds in order to change our reality. Revolution, reaction, fascism, and democracy are obviously not final facts. They are cultural products, ways of reaching order by manipulating a universe which is neither all mind deceiving itself, nor all matter acting a dumb show, but a realm in which our minds are creatively in contact with matter and with other minds.

To "explain" mind or culture by any simple mechanism grounded in matter is to impose a rigid and angular absolute on the fluidity and variety of experience. Now whoever attacks art attacks mind and, through it, conscience and morality, which are the cohesive forces of society. He may pretend to launch his attack in the name of science or historical determinism (as we shall shortly see), but he is untrue to both and remains, in Samuel Butler's phrase, the Common Enemy.

The Freudian analysis of the mind is, on the contrary, pragmatic—that is, social and ethical. It is only mechanistic by accidental fiat. The psychoanalysts were indeed the first who clearly showed that art could aid in "sublimating" the irrational instincts. The word sublimation, with its uncertain meaning, is unfortunate. It suggests a "forgetting of the lower in the pursuit of the higher" when there is no high or low but only organization or disorder. The arts serve us socially by organizing our thoughts and emotions as well as by extending our vicarious experience. The device is not automatic; a kind of work is required for us, but that work, as Freud points out, leaves beneficent traces in our system. Seeing the world through the eyes of a powerful thinker, be he Butler, Goethe, or Karl Marx, makes us see its contours in sharper relief. So far from being an escape or an illusion, the artistic experience is a test of our senses and imagination. We may be "color blind" but we can at least learn from art that differences and distinctions exist where we saw only a blank surface.

What Freud and other psychologists legitimately combat in our culture is the merely verbal, the abstractions, the oversimple formulas, the one-piece dogmas of the kind I have been examining in these pages. Applied to the political world, this same psychoanalysis convincingly shows that it is the *misdirection* of strong impulses that gives rise to anti-intellectualism and activism, to the fear of being unrealistic, and the hue and cry about imaginary escapists. The impulses themselves are normal and inevitable, a conclusion which, far from being discouraging, only brings us face to face with our responsibilities. If there be any escape it is the refusal to use our minds steadily and concretely, it is the reaching out for ready-made standards as substitutes for individual judgment. The most popular of these short cuts is of course the superstition of race, which combines all the elements I have so far catalogued as the enemies of democratic culture. It must consequently be attended to as the epitome of absolutist thought. It will also by its nature serve to lead us from the realm of art, which is one instrument of democratic pragmatism, to science, which is its complement.

7   The "Race Mind" to End Mind

RACISM sits enthroned to-day as a world power because it feeds on our most inward and familiar feelings. It expresses our vigilant concern with culture—for does not racialism sit as a judge on the products of minds? It claims for itself absolute validity, for we want a sure test to apply with a view to taking action. It thwarts none of our other prejudices, for it wears the mantle of science, which is the garment of our most authentic magicians. And it has the decisive appeal: its simplicity. If good and bad qualities are transmitted by race, we no longer need to think about personal conduct. We must merely purge the nation on the principle that a race brother can do no wrong and an alien can do no right.

Unfortunately there is no agreement about what constitutes a race or what its distinctive signs are; which puts us at the mercy of any group that finds it convenient to separate the sheep from the scapegoats on arbitrary lines of their own. Long before things get to that stage, however, the habit of race-thinking has gangrened our minds, played havoc with our culture, and made us ready for the familiar acts of indiscriminate cruelty. We may abhor the idea of harming those who have done us no harm, but if we are told long enough that our neighbor's peculiar racial mind is a disintegrating ferment in our civilization, we begin to look upon him with an altered eye. The first unaccountable mishap in our lives will seem the proof of his evil influence, and we shall be ready to murder him with a clear conscience.

I have said that race-thinking to-day is a world-wide phenomenon, which may have seemed an overstatement. That appearance is due solely to the fact that we make a distinction between those who have race *prejudices* and those who, without prejudice, use the idea of race to explain this or that. The distinction is individually important; socially it is not, for in a moment of crisis it would be obliterated by a universal rally around the idea of race. It is the reality of that idea in the democratic mind that concerns us here. The portentous sign of it is that one cannot open a book, a newspaper, or an advertisement without finding race-thinking in it, expressed or implied. The commonest form it takes is the race label —that is, the description of something or somebody as Latin, Aryan, Teutonic, and so forth. The impression conveyed is that something illuminating has been said. Here is a sample:—

> It has been said that Delius paralleled Debussy in giving expression to the movement now known as "Impressionism," only that while Debussy represented the Latin races, Delius represented the Teutonic and Celtic.[1]

The question whether there is any scientific truth in racial theories cannot be argued here. I have elsewhere shown* that historians and scientists who keep their eye on all the available facts repudiate every race theory yet devised. Mankind can be divided into distinct races only by someone who deliberately shuts out contradictory evidence, or who is blinded by surface likeness to underlying diversity. It might be argued that to look at a single aspect of reality for a given purpose is pragmatically sound. The trouble is, it neglects consistency and completeness, which are important parts of practicality. Blindness to facts leads to sudden collision with them, which is by definition unpractical.

* In *Race: A Study in Superstition* (1937; 1965).

Whether it be a strict race system or only a loose verbalism as in the example quoted above, race-thinking is an attempt to judge of difficult matters in an easy way. A people's art, science, philosophy, or government is "explained" by referring to the racial origins of the group. A man's qualities are summed up by a single allusion to his origins.* In both cases, racism fails to do what it pretends to do, which is to inform us fully and accurately about the matter in hand. The appraiser is looking, not at the pearl necklace, but at the owner's visiting card.

In common usage, the racial "cause" can be discovered in the subject's birthplace just as well as in his parentage, but the seemingly solid material base makes the inference no better. It is still magic. Perhaps its utmost magical power can be seen in Hitler's claim of pure racial impenetrability: "It is a fundamental principle that no man can possess a deep appreciation of a cultural product which is not rooted in the very nature of his ancestry. [Stormy applause] . . . It is certainly possible to respect the works of art of another people, but they are bound always to remain unintelligible to our deepest self."[2]

Even though one does not push racial purity to this degree of exclusive denseness, the tendency is and remains exclusive in effect. One may think that calling Debussy a Latin and Delius a Celt adds to our imaginative perception of their work; actually it subtracts from it by putting an empty word over a concrete experience. The racial term is an extinguisher thrown on the composers' light and on ours.

The reason for this is inherent in the nature of classification. A good classification requires that the definition shall hold exactly true of all members of the group,

---

* In Germany even mathematicians have been divided into "races" according to the tendency of their mathematical speculations. Music being the most plausible "sign of race," by virtue of its instinctive and emotional elements, I shall continue my argument with musicological examples. See Eichenauer, *Musik und Rasse.*

and not of the members of any other group.[3] This is an ideal seldom reached even in the natural sciences, but its purport is inescapable: classification stresses similarities, common denominators, and residues; it disregards differences, individuality, and fullness of being.

Even if a biological race existed and if Debussy could be proved to belong to it, it would only tell us something that we are not particularly eager to know. In dealing with him as an artist, we take it for granted that he belongs to the anatomical classification, Man. If he were physically deficient—deaf or one-armed—the irregularity might deserve our attention on biographical grounds. But it is this very kind of irregularity that the racial classification fails to bring out. It can only group identical things to the extent that they are identical, or very similar. Calling Debussy a Latin means, if one puts the best construction upon it, that some ancestor of his served in Caesar's legions, and came to settle in Gaul rather than in England or Spain.

If "Latin" is used still more loosely to signify in a vague way the culture of France, then we have taken a great deal of pseudo-scientific and pseudo-historical trouble for nothing. We must begin all over again with other terms in order to describe, not Latinity, but modern French culture and its effects.[4]

Even such a description of national culture, appropriate as it may seem, belongs to the useless pattern of race-thinking. It is but another form of the confusion between cause and condition. Because we observe a certain similarity among the works of art made by the Dahomey Negroes and a certain though lesser similarity among the works of art produced by the English, we jump to the conclusion that the similarity in each case is due to their belonging to the same physical group or to having the same color of skin. But the similarity in art could be correlated equally well with a great many other factors common to each group: they eat the same food, wear the same clothes, worship the same gods, speak the same language, and tell the same tales. "Exactly," reply a good many racists, "that is what we mean by race. Human culture depends on physical factors that bring likeness into everything emanating from the particular group. Race can mean nothing else but the transmission of all these factors and their effects by way of generation. In other words, Race = Culture."

The story by now is a little confused. Do the racial germs get transfused into cultural works apart from environment? That is, does environment exert no direct effect on art, or must it first "get into the blood"? If so, how long does that take? Do these factors of blood and environment all act at once, inevitably, or is there a chance sorting out of causes and effects that makes a particular totem pole or poem what it uniquely is?

Two different racial theories are obviously intertwined here: the wholly mystical one of blood and soil (parentage and birth), which does not bother to trace out particular consequences but acts in a lump to make all "Aryan architecture," for instance, one and the same art; and the mystic-materialistic one which tries to hook up particulars to their antecedents and gets involved in refinements such that the forty counties of England hardly suffice to account for all the "racial types" of art produced on English soil.*

This particularism (in a double sense) is bound to mislead. The racist who says that race is culture and that culture dictates what the individual artist or thinker will do is implicitly admitting that he does not know which factors or combination of factors are going to form a given artist or work of art. The Dahomey Negroes may have a single culture but modern nations have heterogeneous cultures. It is not true that all Englishmen eat

* For example, in Havelock Ellis's *Study of British Genius.*

the same food, wear the same clothes, worship the same gods, and tell the same tales. And as we might expect, the permutations of their religious, class, and dietary differences produce an endless variety of art forms that are all entitled to the epithet "English." Instead of a roulette wheel with only one number that invariably comes out, the materialistic racist must admit virtually infinite possibilities. Getting the artist's number thus becomes a much more complicated task than ordinary race labels, denoting a few stiff categories, can encompass. And what is true of the artist or thinker is true of any group or individual in the nation.

2

The purely mystical racist, as we have seen, has not even a case to defend. His explanation amounts only to saying "Race does it" and stopping short. Totalitarian racism has generally combined the two methods, but when argument is needed it puts forth national or historical traditions as the embodiment of race. We then have Race= Culture=Nation.[5] Indeed for most people everywhere, race and nation are interchangeable—as can be seen in the Debussy-Delius comparison already quoted: the writer has translated Debussy's French *nationality* into the supposed Latin *race,* and Delius's into the Teutonic and Celtic. It is the uncertainty about English racial origins, or else Delius's German parentage, that accounts for the absurdity of his getting a double dose of race.

Now, the modern nations are artificial groups made fairly recently by political history, and not "in the beginning" by natural history. Before the French Revolution a poet could still boast on the title page of his book that he was from Calais,[6] and the only last names we use for Raphael and Leonardo are those of their birthplaces. Such small towns have for us to-day no racial or intellectual significance, but less than one hundred years ago in disunited Italy the name of every town stood in its neighbors' eyes for some special vice—a racial characteristic of each inhabitant.

If it was "true" then why is it not so to-day? By what magic have the failings and virtues of the town passed to the modern national states numbering millions of souls? The probability is all the other way: living together in a small town might conceivably make people's ·characters alike; belonging to the same nation does no such thing. Besides, the laws of chance suggest that in any million people most, if not all, kinds of human character must be found. It is noteworthy that every language has words to describe every kind of temperament. Stupidity, logic, or excitability cannot belong to a group as if that group had a monopoly of it—a monopoly distributed evenly among its members and excluding its opposites.

But suppose it possible to define races in this sense and so discover a test of race: it would still be impossible to apply consistently. When a man's ancestry is, as we say, mixed, whose racial germ shall we choose? Race-minded biographers seek out great-aunts, paternal grandfathers, and dominant mothers, who presumably gave the subject his character, but all that is ever offered as evidence is a vague similarity, snatched here and there from letters and diaries. If the grandfather had a bad temper and the grandson likewise, the critic instantly cries "Heredity!" But many people have quick tempers without being on that account cousins, or blood relations, or geniuses of the same race. The connection is to be proved, and the proof is always missing. Moreover, temper, like all human qualities, is a great variety of things under one name. It is difficult to judge of its causes, appearance, and amount, and even more difficult to differentiate them in words.

It is no doubt because of these difficulties that the national and racial adjectives are made so much of in art criticism and politics. They seem to add something, to stop the gap of ignorance. It sounds expert to refer to the artistic soul of a Slav or French clarity and logic. But these, whatever the mystics may say, are nothing more than artistry, clarity, and logic taken by themselves. Only those Slavs who are artists have an artistic soul, and the way that soul differs from that of other artists is in speaking Russian, dealing with Russian themes, and acting generally like other Russian *non-artists*. To juxtapose the two sets of characteristics fails utterly to state what and how much of any given mental quality is present in, say, Tolstoy, and how his "soul" differs from Dostoyevsky's or that of a moujik.

The racist sometimes sees how hopeless is his attempt, and contents himself with a bare indication of an author's parentage. Then having limited heredity most unscientifically to the immediate forebears, he draws critical conclusions which rest on a reading of the author's birth certificate rather than on a reading of his works. A comparison of several biographies of the same man is enlightening in unexpected ways. Berlioz, for example, is by turns "pure French," "Germanic," "essentially Gallic," "Latin," "Gascon," "part Italian," "of southern temperament," and "strongly Nordic."[7] When so much has been said, nothing has been said. The biographer who would try to explain what these phrases mean would be wasting time that he should devote to a direct description of his subject's life and character.

It is in the nature of cultural things that they will strike each beholder differently, and no one can blame the critic or biographer for bringing out what is nearest his heart or what he may feel has been undervalued or overlooked. But one can blame him for pinning an ambiguous label on his discovery and pretending that the formula of a rare compound has been given.

Feeling his inadequacy the racist tries to bolster up his

nomenclature with references to climate or scenery. For example, the writer already quoted on Delius goes on to say: "His mood pictures . . . give an impression of North European nature not to be found elsewhere in music." What North European nature may be is even vaguer than Celtic or Teutonic. And one is further puzzled by knowing that Delius, born in England, lived most of his life in France, after several years' sojourn in Florida and Southern Germany. Is one to suppose an "atavistic yearning" for the Norselands that Delius never inhabited?

It is of course the critics, the public and certain politicians who go in for racial and geographical labeling. Most artists are too busy absorbing and organizing experience to pay much attention to origins, whether genetic or geodetic. When an artist like Flaubert or Nietzsche does seem to support some such national or racial classification of culture, it is usually found on closer examination that (*a*) he frequently contradicts himself and (*b*) he has a purpose, generally aggressive and impatient, for committing the fallacy. He is picking up the nearest club and wielding it, not in behalf of his own "race" or against his own culture, but in behalf of culture as a whole against the Philistines. He temporarily associates the latter with his own nation because it is his fellow nationals that he knows best and hates most. Flaubert's desire to think himself a Norman Viking, and Nietzsche's pride in his Polish ancestry, are to be read as contempt for the French (Latin) Philistines of the 1850's, and the German (Teutonic) Philistines of the 1870's, respectively. So far from these names indicating profound differences of "soul," they reveal an identical attitude in two artists at odds with contemporary society.

3

Still, many persons who are tolerant and cultivated maintain that they *feel* cultural differences along national lines; that there is something essentially French; that such a novel could not have been written anywhere but in England. These three statements only appear to be the development of a single idea. They correspond in fact to distinct feelings and inferences. It is undeniable that there is such a thing as cultural traditions but these are only the conditions not the cause of art. Tradition may or may not produce a family likeness among works done in one nation or at one time. Traditions die out and are replaced by new ones. To forget this and imagine a national continuity stronger than any other cultural force is the error that underlies racist criticism.

We fall into it because we are influenced by language and allusions to things that we know beforehand to be English, German, or French. We tend moreover to consider only a given slice of the national tradition. Rabelais is as French as Racine, but would we guess it from their works alone, language aside? The style and mind of Shakespeare are as entitled to the name English as Pope's, but has their common national origin produced any deep similarities of temper, outlook, diction, form, or contents? The fatally easy thing to do is to set up in oneself an absolute of what is "essentially" English and proceed to throw out whatever does not square with it. It may indeed give a residue of pure Englishness, but it fails entirely to support the original contention, which was that whatever is English, of any period or style, is more like itself than it is like French or German work of the same kind.*

* George Bernard Shaw exposed the fallacy half a century ago: "Grieg . . . is a 'national' composer. . . . I am not to be imposed on by that sort of thing. I do not cry out 'How Norwegian!' whenever I hear an augmented triad; nor 'How Bohemian!' when I hear a tune proceeding by intervals of augmented seconds; nor 'How Irish!' when Mr. Stanford Villiers plays certain tricks on subdominant harmonies; nor 'How Scotch!' when somebody goes to the piano and drones away on E flat and B flat with his left hand, meanwhile jigging at random on the other black keys with his right. All good 'folk music' is as international as the story of Jack the Giant Killer or the Ninth Symphony." (*London Music in 1888–1889*).

Nationalism, which is thus being erected into an absolute, is a thing of the last three or four hundred years; but in proportion as the sentiment of nationality has grown, the means of communication have kept pace. They have neutralized what might have become large-scale provincialism in culture. The result has been that likeness can be found in ideas and works of art produced in widely separated countries. Individual artists have borrowed freely across time and space from other men and other traditions.

The same Debussy, for example, who "represents" for our racial critic the "Latin" countries, was greatly influenced by the Russian school. They, in turn, were affected by their own (Slavic) folk tradition, the German (Teutonic) musical grammar of the eighteenth and nineteenth centuries, and the individual style of (the multi-racial) Berlioz, who visited Russia twice during the course of the century and left his mark on Debussy's models, Moussorgsky and Rimsky. In addition, Debussy was greatly attracted to Spain and its folk tunes. He was sensitive to poetry and his mind took the imprint of Flemish poets like Maeterlinck, Italians like d'Annunzio and Rossetti—or is Rossetti an Englishman?—and French ones like Mallarmé, whose obscure verse hardly fits in with the "essentially French" tradition of clarity and logic. All of these plus the unknown and unknowable influences of schooling and personal history formed the mind of Debussy. No doubt he had things in common with other French musicians like Massenet and Ravel, but these men, looked at biographically and critically, are again unique products of their own background and environment.

To trace the interconnections and similarities among artists is a legitimate part of criticism, but it is no part of criticism to attempt to blur the differences that exist, in a vain attempt to find common denominators and racial formulas. The attempt is proved vain not only because it has failed again and again, but because the true common denominator of French music is simply the notes of the scale, just as the true common denominator of English poetry is the Oxford Dictionary. Everything else is individual, unstandardized, induplicable, which is the reason we value it.

4

One other motive, as was said earlier, often incites to race thinking—the desire to be scientific. The belief is strong that mental products can be reduced to physical or material causes; we saw one of its results in the false psychoanalytic criticism discussed in the last chapter. Race seems to supply a physical explanation for the features of art and thought.

The same considerations refute both fallacies. The mind is undoubtedly related to the body and affected continuously by it from birth till death. No one questions the fact, and no one should think of replacing a crude materialism by an equally crude idealism which would make of culture a floating spirit, blowing nobody knows whence or whither. The man of art or science is not a machine and neither is he a megaphone. The skeptic about race is consequently not against science but against a crude imitation of science. He demands that attention be paid to *all* the physical elements in the cultural situation: the age, health, poverty, and social position of the artist; his ancestry, his audience, his friends and enemies. These are things that can in most cases be described easily enough. The difficulty consists in knowing how they fit and what they mean. And it is at this point that absolute materialistic criticism breaks down.

It is too simple to say with some Neo-Marxists that a man's views are those of the class to which he belongs. What about Marx himself? It is too easy to say with Möbius that a poet's heredity is from his mother. What about Beddoes? It is too easy to say with Candolle that there is a diagonal axis across Europe along which one can find the greatest geniuses to have been born. The axis did not produce them. These discoveries about art and science are useless. They do not tell us what to see or feel, what to compare, remember, or admire. The world at large has noted a connection between madness and genius, between falling in love and writing poetry; but these observations, like the more rarefied ones of Marxists and racists, are completely off the point. Marx would disown those of his followers who are misled by the term "class ideology"— a collective noun for the many ideas of many people— into thinking that a class is a unified cause like the strepto-coccus.[8] The test of experience shatters the pattern as soon as it is applied. Not every man who falls in love can write like Shelley; not every lunatic like Cowper; not every middle-class journalist thinks like Karl Marx; not every dyspeptic thunders like Carlyle. Therefore other factors must have come into play. Between those other factors and the few that the system-ridden critic condescends to look at there are complex relations which also affect the final result. Dyspepsia does not act by itself as if it were a demon with a mind of its own, yet that is what the pseudo-medical critic, like any witch doctor, makes it out to be. The pseudo-economic and pseudo-scientific critic of every kind treads in the same footsteps and applies the same logic, only the heading is different.

The elaborate apparatus of materialistic criticism amounts to saying: *This* is nothing but *that,* an equation which is always incorrect except in cases of mistaken identity. It is a fallacy whether the *that* is a racial word, a class distinction, a family name, or even an ordinary human motive. And it overlooks one of the most common occur-rences in the history of mankind, namely the way in which what we call genius circumvents material fact, defeats likelihood, and turns handicaps to account. The poet of weak constitution and poor health may write faint elegies or rousing war hymns, or each by turns—there is no telling.

The temptation to materialistic thinking might become less if we expected fewer reasons and more intuition on the part of critics. Our interest in culture has taken the form of asking, "What produced this?[9] How was it done?" We want to find the secret formula. We are afraid of being put upon by imitations. We want to be able to tell the real article by some other criterion than the thing itself. The studies of genius have been informed by the same purpose of "spotting" it by something extraneous to its performance, just as we tell silver by the hallmark because we do not trust our ability to judge of the lustre and workmanship. In a word, the "race mind," however conceived, ends by denying the very function and power of mind. Race discriminations are kept in order to do away with the need to be discriminating, and the elimination of judgment from the cultural life becomes a "scientific" goal, as if culture would retain its value in a world where you could test it by formula and litmus paper.

There has also been a desire to belittle the greatness of genius and the value of art by showing them to be by-products of mental derangement, nationalism, heredity or class interests. In all these fancies, as in the discovery of the racial germ or cultural "axis," the mark of absolutism is clearly visible. The search for the absolute best, the true, the racially safe, the only art, rewards nothing but vanity. The profoundly practical use of the fine arts as sustenance and succor is given up in favor of their use as a sign of superiority. And by a fitting poetic justice, this irrelevant pride has deadened sensitivity. Snobbishness, racial repudiation of "alien" cultures, "elimination" of periods and persons—these are the final fruits of pseudo-scientific materialism in talk about art. Translated into political action, it means the end of democratic many-sidedness and the beginning of totalitarian tyranny.

But if that is the work of pseudo-science, of mechanistic materialism, of inconsistent race theories, what is science itself, divested of its false social implications? The question follows unavoidably from what precedes. Having seen the failure of the materialistic absolute in criticism, psychology, and art, we must now disentangle science, a pragmatic method, from materialism, a simple and inadequate absolute.

8 Science, Social Science, and Pseudo-Science

WHAT science is and how it can be applied to the study of culture, what history and the other social sciences can tell us about civilized life, are inquiries properly put to anyone who throws doubt upon materialistic absolutism in all its forms. It would be presumptuous at this late date to "explain what science is," in a literal sense, to a public that has been science-lectured nearly to death. I have no such intention, but only that of offering a few hints about what science does. If we think, as Freud mistakenly thinks, that science copies the external world, we are bound in the end to join hands with the materialists, embracing the consequences that we have seen and rejected. If we do not think that science is an exact, unchangeable, guaranteed facsimile of the outer world, then we are empirical pragmatists and can remain believers in human freedom.

Unfortunately the great democratic public is unwittingly made thoroughly materialistic from the cradle. It speaks the language, like M. Jourdain, without knowing it. Gorged on gadgets which it mistakes for science, it worships its idol, confident that an oracle encased in chromium plate cannot lie. Hence the ease with which the popular mind distinguishes between science and scholarship. Science it regards as absolute truth having to do with the mysteries of the physical world. Scientists are persons of infinite sagacity who come out of the laboratory to tell us that the world is spinning towards the spiral nebulas at an incredible rate. Scholarship on the other hand, is some sort of dry-as-dust occupation which has to do with the Diet of Worms or the Poetry of Greece, and which cannot possibly do anybody any good.

Why the spiral nebulas seem nearer to the man in the street than the poetry of Greece is not at all due to the speed with which we are approaching the one and receding from the other. It is the effect of several confusions: first and worst, the confusion created by the social scientists and their quarrels; then the confusion born of the long warfare between science and religion, which ended by the religious spirit becoming attached to science for want of an intellectually decent shelter in theology; lastly the confusion between scientific method, on the one hand, and the ways of historians and economists on the other.

Although the scientific method is often spoken of with unbecoming reverence, it is at bottom a very simple thing. It consists, ideally, in the observing, and if possible the measuring, of certain effects under controlled conditions.[1] Everything else—instruments, facts, and theories —is either an aid, result, or idea connected with the scientific method. The scientific method is bound up with the technique of experiment. As a method it cannot arrive at the truth by itself, any more than a method for playing the piano can achieve the making of music by itself. There must be behind each a human purpose. But while method must not be divorced from practice, it has proved a cultural stumbling block to lump together as one compelling miracle the *method* of science and the *conclusions* based on experimental results.

But first a few more cautions: scientific "laws" are pieces of thinking which follow (or sometimes precede) the application of the method, but are not the method itself. Again, the virtues which science requires—patience, accuracy, thoroughness, and honesty—are not the method itself, nor are they exclusively possessed by scientists. Lastly, the scientific assumptions, such as the uniformity and continuity of nature, are not "truths," but pragmatic beliefs designed to extend the usefulness of the experimental method.*

But surely, it will be objected, science means something more than the technique of experiment. Do we not speak of science as the body of verified knowledge about the physical world? And are there no sciences, called social sciences, which likewise accumulate knowledge about man in society? If not, what is the use of continuing to study history, sociology, and economics? And if we suppose it of some use, what method can we follow in this day and age except the scientific method?

It is true that science is used to mean knowledge equally with method, and that it applies to the world of man as well as to the world of nature. It is also true that the two bodies of knowledge do not affect us in the same way. Science works; social science talks. We cannot point to the "laws" of social science. Belief in what passes for the laws of social science remains a kind of partisanship; and whereas a knowledge of physical science inspires awe and modesty in others, a knowledge of social science arouses only anger and the spirit of contradiction.

Because of this distinction between science and social science, the modern tendency is to think that a *real* scientist is the man to help us. Many socially aware scientists gladly respond with advice about eugenic marriages, diet, and religion. But even then we are not satisfied, and in spite of their having a professional corner on the truth, we seldom trust them far enough to do as they suggest.

* Without the assumption that nature is uniform and continuous, no amount of experimenting with a column of mercury done on this continent would suggest that a barometer might work in Kamchatka, and no amount of experimenting done anywhere would suggest that the barometer would work to-morrow morning. For further proofs of the pragmatic nature of science, see Note 1.

Hence the contemporary questions—is Marxism, is psychoanalysis, is economics, is history, really scientific? In other words, where can we find absolute warrant for our beliefs? Whom can we trust among the many who proclaim social panaceas in the name of science? Perhaps the best answer is to retrace the path by which history, the earliest of the social studies, became a social science and generated all the others.

We do not have to go back very far. Between 1750 and 1850 the method of the physical sciences, which had been doing well for at least two centuries, began to receive popular attention, thanks to the triumphs achieved in transportation, manufacture, and communication. This tangible success in the control of nature was not due to scientific method alone but to its conjunction with other forces, but in their joy the populace and the educated alike failed to sort out causes and began to think of the scientific method as universally applicable and beneficent.

About the same time (1750–1800), for other reasons too numerous to set forth, the idea spread that man should be studied not as a special creature, but as one of the animals. It was argued that since man grows and dies like other organic forms, so aggregates of men have an organic life. As tribes and nations are organisms, so ideas, institutions, and customs are also natural products, and history is the record of their natural life. What followed this chain of reasoning can be easily imagined: histories were rewritten. National development and the description of customs replaced the tales of kings and battles. Instead of a dim and sketchy past, each nation acquired an ancient and respectable past stretching into "the dark backward and abysm of time." The older books did not contain the materials for the "New History," so search had to be made in archives and cellars for neglected evidence. Tons of records and documents were unearthed, catalogued, and printed.

Libraries hoarded them. Scholarship became a form of devotion to mankind, for it now promised to bring forth the laws of society.

In this mass of new materials much was doubtful, conflicting, obviously biased or forged. How discover the truth and reduce the chaos to an order from which might emerge a scientific history? The obvious solution was to use the scientific method. But if the scientific is the experimental method, it cannot be applied to history. The historian cannot reproduce the effects he wishes to observe, much less control the conditions he describes. He cannot even, like the astronomer or geologist, compare distant though recurring phenomena. The historian had to content himself with adopting as his method the ancillary virtues of science—patience, accuracy, thoroughness, and honesty. He devised ways of insuring their presence by insisting on footnotes, bibliographies, and the rest of the scholarly apparatus. So eager was he that he did not consider whether the result would afford the same kind of certainty as science; but the worthy belief having spread that man could write down history "as it really happened," history was henceforth dubbed a science.[2]

As in physical reasearch, the great task of investigation was divided among many workers. Each man was to do a small corner of his field thoroughly, print his results, and some day by the united effort of many men for many generations, the great laws of history, the guiding principles of mankind, would be established. Germany, in a national awakening from its eighteenth-century dreaminess, gave itself wholeheartedly to both science and history, and, besides producing results of its own, taught the rest of the world how to do likewise.

Before long certain forms of human activity dealt with in histories dropped off the parent "science" and became sciences in their own right. Economics, sociology, government, anthropology, applied the historical method with suitable variations. The results inspired men like Renan to predict the day when there would be no need of art or literature or philosophy: historico-scientific certainty would have replaced these crude guesses, and the truths of law, government, and psychology would infallibly guide human life.

This prediction of more than a century ago seems now a trifle premature. We have had time to notice that whereas the ways of physical science have piled up achievement on achievement, the results of the historical method do not make a sum. They do not compel general acceptance, and the number of rival schools, which grows with every decade, only increases our confusion and helplessness about persistent social problems.

2

Our disappointment cannot be attributed to the over-zeal of nineteenth-century historians. The physical scientists are the first to blame for confusing their own eminently practical method with its results. Not only did they use science as a term of praise, but they used it to mean indifferently the technique, the virtues, the theories, and the laws of science. The truth is that while the technique boils down to manual operations that any person of good intelligence can be trained to do (as Bacon foresaw), the theories and the laws of science are acts of thought that require rare gifts. Overlooking the rôle of genius, the scientist's faith in mechanical technique led to an almost willful neglect of intelligence. And no wonder, for thinking is notoriously difficult and fallible, while manual techniques are a refuge from its rigors. It is easier and safer to determine the melting point of an element than to be Gibbs or Mendeleyev and devise the Periodic Law. It is easier to send out questionnaires and tabulate the results than to have a new insight into human affairs.

The historians argued analogously and belittled thought as "philosophy" or "bias" in order to concentrate on technique, boasting in their pride of impartial scientific results. Impartiality may have been achieved in setting down one "verified" fact upon another, but wherever that occurred, pointlessness was achieved by the same stroke. In time the dissertation, swollen with unorganized facts, came to stand in the public mind, not for science with its useful mysteries, but for scholarship with its useless mystifications, History split in half between the "real scholars" working for the six or eight colleagues engaged in the same specialty, and the passionate, biased men like Carlyle, Michelet, Froude, and Macaulay, who were read by the educated as literature and scorned by the professionals as "unsound." In neither case was the product science.

In the other historical disciplines, the imitation of science came to grief on the same shoals. Physical science has in the main proceeded by division, breaking down into smaller and smaller units the thing to be studied. The aim is to make measurement exact and to sort out causes. But the social sciences deal with man, and man is refractory to division. No sooner has "economic man" been split off by the economist than the same in-dividual (aptly so-called) acts in his capacity as "sentimental man" or "Englishman" and defeats the investigation.

Any reduction of the living being to imaginary units like the atom is falsification,* and in modern society

---

* When we speak of scientific exactitude we imply of course the use of an invariable conventional standard. The "fact" that water boils at 212° F. at sea level is a "conventional fact" in the sense that a degree on Fahrenheit's scale is something agreed upon by convention, for convenience. It does not exist as such in nature and we can make another scale, as did Réaumur. History knows only one kind of conventional fact similar to the many kinds devised by scientists. It says

where the ease of motion multiplies the relations into which man enters, the sorting out of parts is impossible. Physiological psychology, Ricardian and mathematical economics, physical anthropology, all of them describing a single aspect of man, produced the same kind of barren science, true perhaps in Laputa, where tailors make clothes by trigonometry, but not on this pragmatic planet.

Though division and measurement are ruled out, history and the social studies can nevertheless find "truths"; but these truths are of a very different order from those of the physical sciences. Both kinds of truth are pragmatic—that is, are guesses hazarded to fit a perceived reality; but the truths of physical science are alone susceptible of detailed verification and fairly accurate measurement. Yet this difference did not prevent social scientists from borrowing current theories of science, chiefly Evolution, and fitting their facts into the ready-made cubbyholes of Natural Selection and the Survival of the Fittest, thus capping their treatment of man as an animal by making history absolutely and materialistically determined.

From the days of Herbert Spencer to the present, hundreds of histories of everything from morals to music have been built upon this so-called genetic analogy. Not only did it make social science seem scientifically up-to-date, but it helped everybody to "prove" that because the "evolution" of this or that had up to now been thus-and-so, the world was bound to go in a given direc-

---

for example, "Napoleon Bonaparte was born in 1769." The three parts of that statement cannot be distorted or disputed: name, birth, and date are matters of tacit convention. But every other type of historical fact suffers change with every restatement. Compare, for example, the "facts" of the arrest of the five members of Parliament by Charles I in Clarendon, Hume, Macaulay, and John Richard Green—even the conventional word "arrest" is misleading, since the members were not arrested.

tion. Socialism, Anglo-Saxon supremacy, music-drama, and the use of bathtubs were held to be fated from the beginning. The hint to the reader was that he had better fall in with the inevitable course of events or be left behind in an unevolved state. Such histories were both exposition and exhortation, the sternest among them being Marx's *Capital*—an historical masterpiece which the author never tired of comparing with the work of Darwin and which is still printed under the rubric of Science.*

We have come at last to the heart of the error: the desire to establish a scientific determinism in history led to a confusion of materialistic cause with material condition. History can describe conditions fairly accurately but it can never without distortion isolate causes. Evolutionary theories and economic interpretations of history brought out interesting and important aspects of the past, but "proved" nothing and predicted nothing infallibly. The historian could string his facts on the artificial thread of historical "genesis," but he could never show in what way a government or an art form "grew out" of another. He took for granted the biological link among things because the link between father and son is familiar. He chose his facts ahead of time for their suitability to his scheme and stressed the points of linkage, but the critical reader grew skeptical as soon as he picked up another historian of equal competence and found a different evolution with different links and a different outcome "scientifically" shown.

As early as 1875 a number of scientists and philosophers began to protest against the arrogant and confused dogmatism of certain historians and men of science. But the momentum was too great. To this day the warrant "science says" is, at least for the common man, a presumption of absolute truth.

* See the Everyman edition of Volume I.

The educated are gullible too, but they demand the trappings of scholarship before they yield to the same faith. When, therefore, one asks "Is it scientific?" and the answer is "Yes," three things are possible: the magic word may have been used in ignorant appeal to authority; it may denote results obtained and tested by the experimental method; or else it can mean, "This is the best knowledge that intelligent and honest research can produce at this time." In other words, the historical method basic to the social sciences is the alternative to the experimental; it is not its duplicate in the realm of human affairs. The limitations imposed on historical truth may be galling, but they cannot be removed by disregarding the difficulty and making futile passes at a science of man.

The reaction against the false gods of social science has just begun. In the Neo-Aristotelians and Neo-Thomists we find a body of men who emphasize the need for logic and who put history and science in lesser niches as fact-furnishing aids to metaphysics.* It is a protest against Renan's dogma that science will gradually supplant present modes of religion, philosophy, and politics, making them empty superstitions by the side of absolute truth. One may question the capacity of Aristotle or Saint Thomas Aquinas to solve our social and economic problems, but one can only sympathize with the demand for philosophic thinking. Whatever pleasant surprises the future may hold for us in the shape of robots and automata, so far the human mind is the only instrument yet found which can make useful judgments in live situations where the ascribing of effects to single causes is impossible. The mind and the mind alone weighs the imponderable and sees through the tangled mass. It often fails, but at least it attempts what is wanted and not some other easier task next door.

* For further treatment of the Chicago School, see below, Chapter 10.

3

Reliance upon the human mind does not mean that the social sciences should forgo instrumental aids. Many devices, from the punched card to the X-ray forgery detector, are at its disposal. So are statistics and other branches of mathematics. But in using these aids it is fatal to forget that judgment and hypothesis come first in order of importance. What we want to know cannot be squeezed out of a machine by throwing in the raw materials at one end and grinding out results at the other. Any investigation, be it a door-to-door canvass, a questionnaire, an historical essay, or a statistical study, starts with definitions and assumptions, expressed or implied, and the worth of these—other things being equal—is the worth of the study. Materialism in social science is therefore inimical to democratic culture. For while a modern nation needs more and more fact-finding studies, it must resist the temptation to let "the facts" substitute for judgment. Responsibility cannot be eliminated from research, under pain of finding the supposedly "objective" results criminally misleading.

The simplest social facts are complex things. When we say "divorce" or "revolution," we are talking about many different events under one name. Any attempt to compare or count such units must be done with a sharp eye for the disparities. Not only do things called the same differ among themselves, but the same things differ in their consequences. Polygamy is hardly *one* social phenomenon wherever found; intelligence is not the same in the jungle and in the Smithsonian Institution. An account that lumps heterogeneous matter under a common name—as we saw in the case of race-thinking —yields in the end less knowledge than a good guess. Tables and curves cannot make up for the original flaw.

Our faith in the conclusions of social science must be

a pragmatic faith; that is, the conclusions themselves must be subjected to the pragmatic test. We must make sure that the facts presented truly relate to the thing studied. Most studies of Genius, for example, are compiled with the aid of *Who's Who* or some such list of names. Now if there is anything certain to the judging mind, it is that the overwhelming majority of the successful people catalogued in *Who's Who* are not geniuses. To say this is not to insult but to congratulate them. The distinguished senators, brigadier generals, and executives are what they are because of qualities diametrically opposed to those definable as genius. Anything concluded about them under that name is not knowledge but fantasy. The fact that *Who's Who* is full of data, whereas geniuses often leave scanty records, is not to the point. As well look in a lighted spot for an article one lost elsewhere, because it was too dark there to find it.

Equally absurd are those studies of "artistic ability" based on tests of sensory perception, which are themselves of doubtful accuracy. The investigator starts with a subject's ability to distinguish one shade of blue from another, or one series of notes from another; records individual scores by adding these "facts" together; finds averages, percentiles, and quotients, and shortly cites exact figures comparing persons, schools, age groups, and races, in respect of a uniform commodity which he has the impertinence to call "artistic ability."

The difficulty of defining terms and interpreting results has led certain economists and sociologists to abandon these obvious statistical ways and to try devising new symbols and "models" for dealing with social affairs. But if the "sociograms" and "econometrics" thus produced are to be of use, they will sooner or later have to be translated back into the terms of actual life. It is unlikely that the scholar who cannot precisely tell what is in front of him can furnish society apt and refined advice. The hope repeatedly expressed at philosophical and scientific congresses that some day men will be able to converse in mathematical terms will mean either that mankind has given up direct contact with people and things, or that life and society have previously been atomized into fixed and interchangeable units.

This lesson has been learned once before in the craniometry and racial anthropology of the last century, which led to ludicrous, and occasionally murderous, results simply because the arithmetical precision of a cephalic index was thought to correspond to something absolute in man. It determined whether he was intelligent or stupid, brave or cowardly, racially elect or racially damned. Because mathematics and biology are "real" sciences, they are not thereby politically useful or wise, and the fallacy of juxtaposition must be guarded against. To hear some scientists who take an interest in social affairs one might think that the fruit fly was the measure of all things; and after reading certain studies in sociology and psychology one would suppose that the only way to gauge human capacities was to put rodents through mazes. In sum, the behavior of apes, insects, and barnyard fowl can only cast a vaguely suggestive light on the human scene. This seems particularly true when we reflect that those who know most about animals have been forced by their specialization to neglect the study of man in history.

The spectacle of a competent scientist talking palpable nonsense about race betterment through war, or of eugenic marriages for the production of able leaders, is always sad. His conception of leadership, culture, and political history is so obviously not that of a well-stocked mind, but rather that of a docile newspaper reader, that his views do not even afford common ground for debate. Pseudo-science of this sort is twice dangerous, because it impresses many who, knowing themselves incompetent to criticize the scientist, dare not carp at the public oracle.[3] If it were not dangerous to lay down rules in these matters, one might affirm in the light of unhappy experience that the only scientist worth listening to about social affairs is the one who does not believe science competent to decide social questions on the basis of physical fact.

4

The mutual sidetracking of science and scholarship in the nineteenth century has had the common result of obliging the modern scholar, historian, or social scientist —whatever name he chooses—to employ his mind and his virtues (for he has no *method* in the proper sense of the word) in the attempt to furnish mankind with guidance. This should not, however, be taken to mean that every book or study must contain a prescription, but that every study, on the contrary, should give up claims to impartiality and certitude, and work out its stated idea or hypothesis; this idea or hypothesis embodying the author's judgment of the human scene as he sees it in the light of historical or other knowledge, and without ogling glances at mathematics or the animal kingdom.[4]

The function of historical thought in a democratic culture is to supply us not only with certain facts, but also with principles for their organization and for drawing tenable conclusions. The whole should moreover be presented with enough art to make it intelligible. We sneer too readily nowadays at the "armchair deductions" of earlier thinkers—Malthus, Carlyle, or Adam Smith; but their errors are outmatched by the footloose fact-finding of modern investigators. It is significant that even for exacting specialists the great achievements still stand: Gibbon, Carlyle, Macaulay, Adam Smith, Karl Marx, compel reading and discussion. Later research may have changed, refuted, supplemented their facts. We edit and correct them. But we find it impossible to substitute "method" for their genius, that is, their power to perceive relations and impress them in a lasting way upon the mind. As John Livingston Lowes puts it:—

> There are few things in the world more interesting than the disclosure of facts which illuminate and throw into fresh perspective a mass of other facts. And the results of research, however learned, may be presented without shallowness or artifice, in lucid order, and with clarity of phrase, and even may at times possess the fascination of a tale. Our fatal blunder is to sit down, when our problem is solved, and let, as we say, the facts speak for themselves. There are few more mischievous fallacies. . . . When we have lived with our own particular chaos of facts for months, it may be for years, we forget with fatal ease that our readers are unfamiliar with the landmarks of anybody's chaos but their own.[5]

Nothing short of such scholarship will do, for the task of social science is to bring both light and order into our neighbor's darkness. If we admit that a fact is no longer true when obscurely put or hidden away in the wrong place, then a mass of "true" facts unorganized, uninformed with narrative life, ceases to function as truth, since no mind, not even the author's, grasps their bearing. It is often said that many an invaluable work has been compiled by a man who never got as far as organizing his materials. If this is ever true, let us thank the author for publishing his sack of notes, but let us not put a premium on such works, or think they add to our knowledge, when it is we who are doing the needful work of producing order. Bricks by themselves will not build a house, and the tragedy of late nineteenth-century scholarship is that so many men devoted their lives to making pyramids of bricks instead of habitable mansions for the spirit.

The fear of being unscientific by making history readable made those men fear Popularization. Contempt for the cheap and easy way is of course praiseworthy, but we must be sure that our praise does not in fact condone indolence and pride. Pride feels that in a democracy mental isolation is splendid isolation; it takes the specialization of the physical scientists for a guarantee of truth; and it enjoys the delusion that a fact—or even the card upon which it is written—is precious for its own sake. William James, whose scientific and scholarly attainments are not in doubt, has some harsh words to say about this attitude. He implies that we should split the time-honored phrase "scholar and gentleman" into two distinct halves:

> At a technical school, a man may grow into a first-rate instrument for doing a certain job, but he may miss all the graciousness of mind suggested by the term "liberal culture." He may remain a cad, and not a gentleman, intellectually pinned down to his one narrow subject, literal, unable to suppose anything different from what he has seen, without imagination, atmosphere, or mental perspective.[6]

This "caddishness" has brought its own retribution. On the ground that truth was esoteric the scholars have let the popularizers capture the public's ear, mislead its mind with facile generalities, and poison its heart with explosive falsehoods. This has been one act of treason by the intellectuals, and it is no accident that the modern world has seen how short a step it is from the scholar's cell to the wider air of the concentration camp. That step once taken under duress, it sounds hardly convincing to complain that the public—by which is meant the relatively small reading public—is unteachable, that its favorite superstititions can never be uprooted, and that our social ills are due to the ignorance of people whom the learned decline to instruct. All that the people seem to have learned after a century of universal scientism is that science is the realm of "wonders" and of absolute certainty, a belief which has merely shifted blind faith from the black-coated to the white-coated priests.

The diagnosis remains easier than the remedy. It is impossible to prescribe the forms of thought that must be joined to the virtues of science—that is, to the historical method—in order to produce good history, anthropology, or economics. This is only another way of saying that history is an art and not a science. Its results are not reducible to formulas but depend for their accuracy upon literary form—art again—while their effectiveness in edifying mankind depends upon a prompt diffusion of ideas.

Social science may have other values for the absolutist, but its primary justification in a democratic culture is pragmatic: ideas and feelings about the historical past and the social present are themselves facts.[7]

The village that voted the earth was flat can be ridiculed or perhaps ignored; but the village that votes for segregation or polygamy is creating a new social fact that cannot be disregarded. Appeals to self-interest alone are of no avail. Technology offers no remedy, unless dropping bombs from an airplane be considered such. The nature of social problems under democracy demands that we rely on persuasion and the diffusion of knowledge. But to prevent an endless war of words that knowledge must be diffused for what it is—a working approximation, a pragmatic handle to reality.

Final truths are denied us, yet if a physicist is not afraid to admit that "science is illogical but not therefore invalid,"[8] the social scientist should not be afraid of his own fallibility and despair of his craft. He lacks the scientist's crutches—experimentation and measurement; and then he is dealing with far more complex problems involving the agency of mind. For this he has the flexible historical method, with its appropriate virtues. Let him use it to the full and affirm: "History is unscientific but not therefore useless." In so doing he will be discharging his duty as a member of a society which relies on a free culture for its maintenance; and he may even help to abate the rampant scientism which underlies race-thinking and which, in scholar-ridden and science-worshipping Germany, made the public mind a prey to the twin absolutes of force and official falsehood.

9   *Absolute Words and Absolute Nonsense*

IF we cannot discover absolute truths, what can we teach that is not essentially propaganda? The answer is: the diffusion of ideas *is* propaganda, whether fascist, communist, or democratic. The democratic hope has always been to raise the threshold of gullibility, to sharpen judgment, by confronting opposite propagandas. And as for choosing—"by their fruits ye shall know them."

The practice of totalitarian regimes everywhere is an acknowledgment that social action depends on the diffusion of ideas. But what is propaganda to you may be Information, Science, Art, History, or the "truths" of social science to me. Even under a dictatorial government there is no avoiding this diversity of outlook, hence the need, in better climes, of critical discussion free from penalties, for the sake of a relatively homogeneous culture. Democracy must therefore accept propaganda and become highly self-conscious about critical discussion.

Propaganda in the derogatory sense is not such an outside virus as we pretend to think. Police states of course rely on fairly low appeals, but all grades of propaganda are compelled to work with common ideas already rooted in western European culture. The official "line" cannot propagate novelties, but must work with established symbols and superstitions—race beliefs, the degeneracy of art, the natural trend of evolution, and the "poisons" of socialism, Christianity, and democracy. Like all ideas these are tied up to strong emotions, and the fact that the emotions can be called forth by using certain words has led to a widespread disillusionment about language as a whole. In an able book by Mr. Stuart Chase we have been made to fear the Tyranny of Words; numberless articles have made us aware of semantics; and, as we saw, scientific students of society have been searching for nonverbal means of communication.[1]

This concern with public debate is democratic and deserving, but the tone of the expounders of semantics is disquieting. We are all agreed that words are slippery things, but the warnings seem to imply: "Words are misleading—don't use them"; or else: "Words color the truth —let us try to give everything its right name once for all and dispose of the ancient difficulty." Either extreme ends in a blind alley. To give up words because they make propaganda possible is like giving up machinery because it can destroy lives. We are once again looking for a scapegoat: this time the dictionary. Or, contrariwise, we must rename freedom, democracy, oppression, because the bare sounds make some people cheer and others hiss. Apparently no one cheers the binomial theorem,* so we must invent formulas of a like sort for dangerous words.

This is to mistake the situation, from popular attitudes to politics and to words themselves. It is to treat words as absolute vessels of truth instead of pragmatic devices for communication.[2] It is to suppose that the hissing and cheering are hidden in the words instead of in the impulsive public mind. It is to imagine that our real difficulties are wholly contained in the words instead of in the world as well.

Words refer to things and are used to call forth some image of the things referred to. Abstractions are only com-

---

* Although Pascal believed that to the mathematician a proposition in geometry becomes a sentiment.

plex collective images which depend for their utility on the imagination of both user and hearer. "Democracy," for instance, is a host of things and ways of behavior, some of which I have been trying to enumerate in this book. If the reader sees a donkey bestrode by Franklin Roosevelt every time I use "democracy," his image is inadequate or perverse, his mind has been cartoon-struck, his imagination has atrophied. The semanticist must not blame me and still less the four syllables in question.

Paradoxically science, cheap printing, and general literacy have made it harder, not easier, for everybody to use the mind's eye and understand words. The noises and sights around us conspire to deaden our imaginations until we take the symbols for the reality. That is what we mean when we cry out that words tyrannize over us. The right words are indeed all-important and we must try to find them, but they will betray us like the wrong words if we are hypnotized by the sound or blind to the image.

It has long been a commonplace of political science that the division of labor in creating anonymity created a great evil. Forgetting that No. 3031 is a man, calling him a "hand," or a "fraction of the annual turnover," are conveniences that we ultimately pay for in cash and calamity. What has evoked less attention is that we are increasingly compelled to deal with people and things in the same fragmentary and abstract fashion—the fragment we abstract and put upon a card. Ours is the Age of Paper par excellence. Modern civilization rests upon foundations of wood pulp, which explains why records are more valued than lives. The first step in any enterprise is to fill out a blank; the next to file it; then to tabulate the lot, print, and circulate more paper, which serves as a surrogate for life.

The city dweller particularly is nurtured on paper during the whole waking day—the newspaper at breakfast, ads in the mail, ticker tape at the office, millions of

records in millions of filing cabinets. We pile up in our
wake a mound of paper which will be for posterity
Pyramid and Sphinx rolled into one. Contact with things
almost disappears. When we are not reducing persons to
formulas, we are busy reducing experience not just to
words, but to set forms of words. We standardize emotions
and events as we standardize the size of nuts and bolts.
The newspaper headline has its own limited diction; the
prose of magazines its uniform style. Each subject has its
jargon, intelligible only to those involved.

Quick communication is our goal, but ready-made
expressions are so numerous, so repetitious and dull, that
we grow callous to their bombardment. We have no
nervous energy left to respond and communication halts.
Advertisements, notices, books, denunciations, make us
weary but no wiser. We accept flood and earthquake as
daily accompaniments to breakfast; the newspaper does
not so much bring the world closer as insulate us from
it. Seeing less and less through the mind's eye we note
fewer and fewer differences. All strikes are splendid or
outrageous just as all Japanese are yellow and sly. We have
the art of putting clichés together grammatically without
troubling the mind. If someone speaks or writes in a
striking way, however clear or simple, we feel a shock as
if rudely awakened, and we understand no better for his
lucidity. We have sunk en masse into the lingo of forgotten things.*

2

In a famous essay published in 1946, George Orwell
analyzed modern political prose as an attempt to conceal

* It is perhaps not too farfetched to suppose that the modern fear
of escapism through the arts and the demand for toughness, cruelty,
real war, and blood in everything from short stories to radio broadcasts
are signs of an attempt to break through the Chinese Wall of words
and rekindle the dying imagination. How it can lead to anything but
the using up of shocks until the worst will seem tame is hard to see.

reality behind a screen of abstract jargon, and he showed that this habit was congenial not only to politicians but also the common non-political man. Loose constructions, fancy reifications, worn metaphors, and inept phrases combine to make the perfect narcotic. The point is worth elaborating and also supplementing. Words, books, teaching, are our sole means of access to nine-tenths of reality. Modern life fixes us in one place, one station, one daily round, and we tolerate this rigidity because of the means which enable our imagination to supply the unknown and the unfelt. If the principal means—standard prose— is failing us through abuse and corruption, we must disinfect it. The task is not frivolous and secondary but central. It is a job not for pedants but for poets.*

Let us look first at the common evils that a little effort would remedy. What makes histories, economic surveys, educational literature, and the daily paper unreadable? Why are people buying more and more picture magazines and lapping up pictorial statistics? What, in short, is killing prose? It is first of all the stringing together of abstract words in place of concrete ones. Abstractions, being vague, suggest extensive "coverage" and absolute meaning, though in fact writer and reader are communing in an indefinite, bottomless drift. Take a sentence: "The method which the word 'technocracy' describes cannot be put into effect without sanctions arising in the political field." Nothing is grammatically wrong; a meaning lurks somewhere, but whole books written in that vein are like a sponge passed over an aching brow: it soothes but leaves a dull head behind.

Our minds—everyone can verify this for himself—are cluttered up with "fields," "areas," "problems," "natures," "conditions," and other abstractions preceded by adjectives and followed by other abstractions interlarded with *of*'s and *to*'s. No one says "To be or not to be"; it is

* H. L. Mencken's *The American Language* is a source of living principles one would like to see more widely exploited.

always "The matter of existence considered *in terms of* a debatable question. . . ." Depersonalization, cowardice —whatever it is, it is bad and it is catching.*

To criticize false abstraction is not to urge a return to the style of the *Edinburgh Review*, yet the famous article that began "This will never do!" had the merit of leaving the reader in no doubt and in a pleasantly wakeful state. Our modern timidity is not all kindness. It is indifference or fear, closely connected with the spread of genteelism— the use of "lady" for "'woman" and "barn dressing" for "manure." Broadcasting stations, it is said, have lists of forbidden words and so censor speech as well as opinion. Among the dangerous words which the radio audience is being spared are those which suggest things, objects, vulgar reality. A physician was forbidden to use the word "body" in a scientific talk, because it smacked of *dead* body.[3] The sense of actuality is threatened, for if its elements are not freely handled in our speech and our minds, it can survive nowhere else.

A second threat comes from the aping of scientific technicality. The child psychologist who writes, "Siblings evince a tendency towards mutually antagonistic responses," when he means "Brothers and sisters often fight," sins against human intelligence and adds his mite to social folly. The intent to be "scientific" is praiseworthy, but misdirected. Physical science uses a special vocabulary of invented words because they are exact and free from irrelevant associations. They are strictly defined and correspond to positive ideas or solid things. When the social scientist takes words like "compulsive," "growth," "attitude," or "adaptation" and uses them as

* The daily verbiage bath makes one immune to such riddles as the following, propounded by the Commonwealth of Massachusetts to any resident who wishes to make his legal residence elsewhere: "Question 17. Has the physical presence of your wife differed substantially from that of yours? . . . (If so, please show on reverse how it has differed.)" (Form 115)

technicalities, yet without definition; when each of his colleagues makes up his own set of terms, borrows others, and mixes them indiscriminately; when the whole "science" is one long sausage string of terminology and nomenclature,* the only excuse for a technical language disappears.[4] The result is barbarism of style and absence of thought concealed behind a simulacrum of science.

I am not arbitrarily singling out a special group: we are all infected with pseudo-scientific jargon. The artist has his machine-age patter, and the rest of us embellish our existence by referring to our "problems," "methods," and "experiments" when none of these things corresponds to what we are doing.† When the family tries a new brand of corn flakes it is an experiment. When the window sticks, we have a method. A fact is not fact but a piece of data: we no longer simply "try" anything. We do not "have a way" with the ladies or with windows. The merest effort is "methodological." The home is a laboratory, the theatre a workshop, the school an experimental unit: life is one long piece of research. Or, to put it another way, closer to the democratic reality, false literacy and science worship have made us into a people of imitative pedants.

3

The threats of pedantry to the public imagination do not affect only the small minority who read books and talk lingo. It may be true that the great mass read the tabloids and continue to be refreshed by such magnificent headlines as:—

* These two words have distinct meanings in natural science, notably in botany. So have "growth" and "development," which in all living things are not synonymous but opposite. Why are these distinctions consistently ignored by psychologists and social scientists?

† An author (not a physical scientist) says of his book that "it is designed primarily as a clinical tool rather than as a research instrument."

POISONED PASTRY FELLS FIVE HUNDRED

But the great mass is subjected to another form of mental drugging which outweighs the benefits of colloquialism. I refer to modern advertising and its next of kin, modern political propaganda. It is necessary to insist on the word "modern," not only because scientific jargon infects them both, but because their latest device is a warp of learned vocabulary upon a woof of nonsense. Nonsense is not something untrue or absurd; it is something that makes no sense. It is the use of words as a narcotic or a hypnotic. It is the logical extension of the lingo, the abstractions, the bathos we have been examining.

The commercial uses of nonsense need not be dwelt on. They are obvious and they have been catalogued by the now numerous defenders of consumer interests.* But the political uses of nonsense have not yet been distinguished from old-fashioned demagogy and mysticism. The Fourth of July oration was patriotic bombast, untrue to fact perhaps, but it did not defy analysis. The mysticism of the French Revolution or that of nineteenth-century Germany was intelligible. The state was deified, war and death were glorious, obedience was the only salvation. The logic of the argument could be disputed, but there was at least an argument to dispute. In fact, nineteenth-century politicians concentrated their best efforts on the popular mind. It was a question of "educating our masters," and though educating generally meant stuffing, the stuff was simple precisely so that it could be grasped.

Now compare any piece of nineteenth-century propaganda with the utterances of our demagogues and see the difference. Two-thirds of what is said is irrelevant or mad.

* The work of these organizations has been useful not merely in saving the subscribers' money, but in educating the educated to distrust the fallacies flavored with science which form a large part of modern advertising.

136

The rest is pedantry. It is mad not in its violence but in its nonsense. It is pedantic in its remoteness from life and love of seeming learned. Explanations of policy are given with such a high scholarly air, such a show of historical and sociological "truth," that the listener who understands not a word feels ashamed to ask questions. Formerly, the Yellow Peril was yellow and one had a vague idea of where it lay. Now race perils are ghostly emanations. They are ideological and metaphysical: one's neighbors are a menace, not only because they arm or threaten, but because they are rationalists and their music is not sufficiently pagan. They fail to hear the soil speaking in their soul as we do. In one and the same utterance, the noble warrior and the tenacious peasant are the one true hero; the Pig is the sacred Aryan animal which acts as a test of race; or yet again Gothic architecture is the true blood bond of the chosen race.* Culture and anthropology, the works of poets and economists, grade-school history and vulgar superstition, are made into a hodge-podge as fantastic and irrefutable as a nightmare.

Nonsense varies with the clime, but only in the different words that are juxtaposed.[5] The very length of the speeches shows that they are not meant to be understood, but to be undergone like hypnotic passes. The old trick of carrying away the mob by appeal to selfish emotions well disguised is replaced by a continuous massaging of the ears with big words. The treatment lasts three hours and, thanks to press and wireless, numbs the senses of the entire nation.

The wonder is not that politicians can be found to

---

* Self contradiction in a flood of words seems to be the fate of eloquent dictators. What Fidel Castro lavishes on the Cubans in 1964 differs only in local subject-matter from what his European models uttered thirty years ago. As one of them remarked to his people, "Had the subject not been really inexhaustible, I should have willingly renounced to address you." (Mussolini, *The Corporate State*, p. 25.)

produce these cataracts of words, but that the populace, always so restless and easily bored, can stand it. How have they been trained to furnish the noisy void with a meaning of their own? It is impossible to say. What is clear is that the educated classes have only themselves to thank for these fruits of compulsory education and cheap newsprint. They have written the textbooks, the editorials, and the popular science. They have made the standards of literacy and been taken in by them. They have educated their masters to a point where soothing nonsense, nonsense absolute, is the key to power.[6] Imagination has died, having first renounced the touch of things. The tyranny of empty words does lead to the tyranny of bodies and souls, but the fault, dear Brutus, lies not in the words but in ourselves.

Every tyranny begins in the mind. It then ferments in culture and reproduces its own image in institutions. Of these, the one at the centre of things, the one which simultaneously receives our culture and perpetuates or alters it, is the school. It is at school that we learn words, hear the first propaganda, develop faith in the printed page, and bow the knee to science. It is there that we are made into thinking minds or gullible automata. But the process is not entirely given up to fate. Education may be faulty, but it is at least conscious of its faults. In the United States particularly, educators have been looking for the agent or the device that makes the difference between the thinking and the gullible mind. What this decisive element may be is still unknown; it is none the less something which at this point we are bound to puzzle our democratic heads about.

10　*What Any Schoolboy Knows:*
A Mystery

THE combined effect of pedantry, gullibility, and scientism which has been sketched in the last three chapters brings us back to its origin in what may be called, for short, low-grade literacy. Compulsory free schooling has been on the statute books for nearly a century, and until recently the West could boast of having literate populations. We meant by this nothing honorific, but a people largely able to read and write. In a mechanized world literacy is no frill. The workman must be able to read "Danger: High Voltage" just as the housewife must be able to fill in the coupon for a free sample. But literacy in this sense is not education; it is not even "knowing how to read" in the sense of taking in quickly and correctly the message of the printed page, to say nothing of exercising a critical judgment upon it. The First World War shocked us into making these distinctions when we saw the results of the army alpha test: it did not so much measure the nation's intelligence as plumb its illiteracy.

In the upper reaches of education, in schools and colleges that train for business and the professions, dissatisfaction did not wait upon a national stocktaking like the army test. Criticism has been continual,[1] reshuffling of methods and curriculum no less so. Those now in charge of education are more than ever aware of the babel of

aims, practices, and results. The machine whirs and
clangs without knowing precisely what it produces. At
times, it clearly fails to train or educate, and seems actually to encourage the extremes of formal stuffing and
slovenly superficiality. The higher grades can build nothing on "What any schoolboy knows," for that is a mystery.
He may know anything from baking nutbread to Relativity, or he may know nothing, from spelling to good
manners.

In the heyday of progressive education four hundred
parents in a town near New York protested to their school
board (it was their protest that furnished the example
above) against a high-school course that included bread-
baking for boys. They demanded a return to the three
R's and thus started a very useful controversy. The in-
cident was reported and discussed as an attack on Progressive Education, but fundamentally the issue was the
one I have just raised—what form of education is adequate for modern life in a democracy? Defending his
school, the superintendent replied that progressive education was not a "system" but was "merely the way he,
as a father and a school superintendent, saw the needs
of the pupils and the way he adapted instruction to meet
them."[2]

Irrespective of system, the double role of school superintendent and father symbolizes the contradictory tasks
of any school in any society: it must prepare the students
for the world as it is, and at the same time it must con-
trive to make a better world to-morrow. The father,
we may say, would have the world better; the superintendent must meet the demands of the *status quo*. The
school must be at once practical and high-minded, not
to say utopian. This is equally true in totalitarian states,
where utopian means the new dispensation of whatever
kind. In the United States a quarter century ago there
were two great movements which, by their awareness

of the social implications of teaching, could be counted on to shape the future of American schools. Progressive Education was one and the agitation for a Return to the Classics was the other.* Both resulted from dissatisfaction with the traditional ways of teaching the three R's, with learning by rote and the lecture method, with the mistaking of "credits" for accomplishment and the snobbish or mercenary motives for degree-hunting. Both movements reflect, though in opposite ways, the impact of science, social science, and the "contemporary chaos."

Progressive education tried to fit education to individual needs. In practice this meant finding out what each pupil is like, what he wants, and what he can do. Hence the use of child psychology, psychoanalysis, mental hygiene, and social statistics. The thought of William James and John Dewey, filtered through academic and pedagogical channels, was the influence behind the practice. Progressive education begins by recognizing individual differences in body and in mind and concludes that education consists not merely in stuffing the mind with facts but in educating the "whole man."

This general plan, despite a new jargon and some new techniques, was anything but new when it began its American career. Every thinker from Plato down has perceived that any education worth the name must make of each pupil a self-propelling person, who not only has learned but can continue to learn. In Aristotle's homely phrase, to educate is not to present the student with a pair of shoes but to impart to him the art of shoemaking.

* It is not robbing Robert M. Hutchins of the great credit due him for championing the classics to point out that the movement with which his name is associated had been gathering strength in America from many sources before the University of Chicago Plan. John Erskine's General Honors course was founded at Columbia in 1919; Meiklejohn's Experimental College at Wisconsin was started in 1928; Flexner's book on universities evinced the same tendency in 1931, and plans for compulsory freshman courses in the Humanities began to be discussed in various leading colleges as early as 1932.

The goal is harder to achieve than it sounds, which is why a progressive education is continually being advocated, being tried, and is ever stiffening again into formal folds from which a new reformer must shake it free. Rabelais complained of Gargantua's formal schooling: "At last his father perceived that truly he studied very well and spent all his time on it and yet profited nothing by it. And what is worse he was becoming dull, crazed, dreamy, and stupid." Gargantua was taken out of school and for a while did nothing but eat, drink, and play silly games. Finally, under a new tutor named Ponocrates, the "whole man" is cared for. Gargantua observes nature, reads, discusses freely, practises the crafts and fine arts, and is trained in sports and good manners. "Thus was Gargantua governed and kept on in this course of education, from day to day profiting . . . which although at the beginning seemed difficult, became a little after so sweet, so easy, and so delightful that it seemed rather the recreation of a king than the study of a scholar."[3]

The ease and delight of study is one of the common criticisms leveled at modern progressive education. It is indeed one of its aims and not so trivial as it looks, for it brings out the divergent views of the world and the school. The world maintains that drudgery, discipline, and conformity are the social virtues par excellence. The school, contrariwise, receives almost from the hand of nature a variety of plastic minds, seemingly gifted with endless possibilities. The school maker's generous imagination shrinks from the thought of forcing these new schools into one shape. Yet the school cannot choose but impose a pattern upon them, even if it is the pattern of having no pattern. Its function is to pour the current culture into young minds, and it inevitably moulds them by rewarding what it thinks fitting.

In a democracy where private schools are free from centralized control, the temptation is great (and yielding to it feels highly moral) to try to change future society by "reinterpreting" the entire cultural heritage and encouraging attitudes at variance with those of the world. Innovations in teaching, subject matter, and discipline follow, and it is at this point that society in the form of four hundred parents protests against progressivism as a mode of schooling.

Nor do the complications stop there. The school finds that although the children have plastic minds, these minds show a wonderful resistance to the introduction of knowledge and the injunction to think. Theoretically, no child problem is insoluble, but practically the problem child is a dynamic fact. There he stands, getting warped, prejudiced, growing daily into a genius or a dunce.

In dealing with him the school is not a solid impersonal block: it is a group of teachers with different habits and opinions. They see the pupils' needs differently and thus make any program, either of conformity or of originality, come out in many different ways. On top of these diversities comes the influence of certain groups, inside or outside the school, who favor particular views, and use all legitimate means of furthering them. Teachers, textbooks, and curricula become the object of a political struggle paralleling that of the world and equally consequential, since the stake is what the commencement speeches refer to as "the citizens of to-morrow."

2

At first sight the individualized education of the progressives seems ideally suited to a democracy where diversity is tolerated and often encouraged. It seems like the thing we have been looking for to make absolutism impossible. But it is soon apparent that an individual absolutism can develop from mere ignorance of what other individuals think. One could argue that democracy is perpetually in danger from an excess of diversity—one-man one-world, and no links with other men and their worlds. We go to school, learn this and that, and issue forth as adults convinced that what we know everybody knows. Our neighbor must then be in bad faith, must be an anti-social egoist, when he disagrees and opposes our excellent plan. The truth is, we do not speak the same language. Communication, as we saw in the last chapter, is becoming more difficult. For words can only be defined by using other words and pointing to situations felt in common. A common background, it seems, would afford democracy a greater chance of success. It would bridge many a gap among educated men; at the very least it would make possible intelligent disagreement in good faith.

Firmly convinced of this, educators at Chicago and elsewhere have hit upon the classics, the great books of the Western world, as the fitting subject matter for a common education. The most thoroughgoing step taken in that belief has been the curriculum of Saint John's College, Annapolis, which consists of reading under supervision a hundred great books in four years.[4]

To many people the word "classics" brings a shudder, and the prospect of four years spent in reading such books would make them prefer for their sons the life of a mechanic to the life of the mind. To others this concentration on the written word, the purely literary tradition, seems a retreat from modernism, by which they mean modern science, the fine arts, and social science. The return to the classics does show a disillusionment with the educative value of science and social science. Relying on the humanities assumes that our cultural heritage in book form contains and will impart all the useful modes of thought that an educated man requires.

It is the basic assumption of the French *lycée* and it has much to recommend it.[5]

If the scientists and the artists feel left out they can truthfully be told that they have only themselves to blame. They did not heed William James's advice about the cultural value of teaching any subject—geology or music—historically. They chose to stand on their own ground as specialists, with the result that science teaching, which forced its way into the curriculum in the last century, and art teaching, which did the same in our day, have produced only scientists and artists, and not educated men conversant with science and art. As for the social sciences, despite their immediate utility, they have been taught as academic disciplines and have produced, not enlightened laymen, but scholars and professionals. To the layman the social question is, "Here are problems, what shall we do?" and he feels not unjustly that instead of throwing their students into premature research, to sink or swim as they can, teachers should first answer the question: "Here are students, what shall we teach?"

It must be said for the classics that they do furnish an answer, positive and practical. What do the classics teach? They teach—to take superficial benefits first—the use of common words and references. An educated man should be able to use the shorthand of thought that literature and history supply. He should understand what is meant by Gordian knot or *le mot juste;* he ought not to think the Copernican Revolution was a Polish uprising. And he should know this vocabulary of ideas, not from a Handbook of Culture, bought to impress family and friends, but from familiarity with the environment of related ideas; it is the context, not the word, that matters.

When not limited to Greek and Latin authors, the classics teach the continuity and the persistence of intellectual and social problems. They show how to understand and enter into the immediacy of the past in order to cope with the present, instead of assuming, in E. J. Lowell's phrase, "that human reason began about thirty years ago."

A classic, the argument runs on, is a book remarkable for the amount of thought and artistry packed into it. It displays in a unique order, with strong emotion and often with beauty of form, many facts and ideas; it educates the feelings by banishing chaos and the mind by clearing it of cant.

Finally, the humanities (as their name implies) put first and foremost what belongs properly to man. In them man is the measure of all things. What is good and bad, beautiful and ugly, useful or useless, is what men find such or infer that God made so. Alone among books the classics are books for any man to read, not for man as scholar, lawyer, or mining engineer.

The contrast between progressive education and the cult of the humanities is clear. The humanities offer a uniform substance to fill the mind, disregarding both "individual needs" and the demand for specialized training. The classics would produce an intellectual class that knows how to think, how to live, and possibly how to govern. The rest of mankind will take care of itself and furnish the men of science and art in the usual way.

Progressive education, on the other hand, takes the pupil as it finds him, discovers his gifts and inclinations, and tries to equip him for a life of art, science, journalism, or business—almost any kind of life except a life of crime. Progressive education would at the same time slowly remould society by altering the individual's response to it, making him more sociable, more tolerant, more diversified in his interests.[6] Progressive education is working for a self-governing egalitarian democracy; the humanists are working for a democracy of the English or French type, where the term "elite" does not necessary mean

146

birth or wealth, but very definitely education and back-ground.

Both these tendencies in America are relatively new but they have spread rapidly. Their proponents have enthusiasm, great talents and great sincerity, and what-ever criticism they may deserve, no doubt can be cast on their seriousness or sense of responsibility. It is as yet too soon to pass final judgment on the contribution each has made to the present scene, but it is not too soon, taking relativist democracy as our measure, to detect errors and record disillusionment.

3

Some of the objections to progressive education are matters of common report. One parent admits that his child is kept interested at the progressive school and that he learns many things; but he cannot, at the age of ten, read or write easily, and his manners are shocking—these lacks being due to the absence of any standard and the fear of repressing individuality.

In the progressive colleges, the objection is to teachers who try to settle the student's private emotional as well as intellectual problems. Likewise the process of pur-posely "dejecting" the student which one college is sup-posed to initiate is considered a nuisance, while the insistence on "growth"—that is, improving in all-round fashion with respect to oneself—is criticized as unjust or as unpractical. It is unjust to the individual who cannot "grow" at will, and unpractical because the world expects more tangible accomplishments than growth.

Where the facts support these objections, they are per-fectly justified: educating the whole man is a worthy aim, but it is delicate and dangerous. Good intentions and the august name of science do not suffice to make a teacher, and using the uncertain psychologies of the moment may cause irreparable damage to both teacher and taught. No one denies that a child in good health and with good eyesight will be a better pupil than one physically and emotionally ailing, but the preoccupation with health and emotion can go beyond its goal and take up a disproportionate share of everybody's time. It then becomes an end in itself, a pious absolute whose right name is coddling, morbidity, or meddlesome interference.

Striving after science also leads to that repellent feature of progressive education which alienates the unprejudiced outsider. I mean the use of jargon to refer to everyday matters; subjects or branches of learning have disappeared; there are only "areas of concentration." Books, pictures, and music are not the simple and good things they once were, they are "exploratory materials." A student does not get on better, he "adjusts"; nor does poise improve—"security solidifies."

Seemingly harmless, these affectations betray a loss of direction, a confusion of means and ends. Often, the scientism goes with a feeling of angry superiority over the older institutions of learning. This blind hostility invents out of whole cloth two absolute creeds where none existed before. Imagining that they are on trial, progressive teachers become defenders of a new faith that requires quasi-theological disputations within their own clan. Should a student with a "theoretical mind" be forced to do "factual work" or encouraged in theorizing? Such mouthings are felt as "problems"; they have "solutions" and teachers must argue until they find them.

This unexpected scholasticism forgets that good teaching is an art, like playing the violin, which after a certain point defies analysis and transcends technique. The teacher is as much a whole man as the student; he can scarcely be expected to remould his personality after each faculty meeting that discusses methods. As a well-known and very successful progressive teacher ironically said after such a meeting: "Let us all agree that we will teach what we can."

Because teachers who give out "dry" or "mere" information are largely useless, it is too lightly assumed by some progressives that subject matter is of no consequence. Yet to replace the lesson in a given subject by an unauthorized and unqualified kind of psychiatric interview is a grave responsibility. When all is said and done about personal problems, tactful help by the teacher in dealing with the usual school subjects not only remains the best form of teaching but also gives the student the clearest perspective on his troubles. Disappointments, obstacles, inferiorities, are part of human experience; they must be minimized, not eliminated from the school.

Teachers who, in the hope of settling everything, forget to teach run the risk of having the student complain in the words Orlando applied to his brother: "I . . . gain nothing under him but growth; for the which his animals on his dunghills are as much bound to him as I." Teachers cannot be at once teachers, psychiatrists, medical men, and social reformers; they waste precious time whenever they fret themselves and their charges over questions that are social in origin and that no teacher and no school can solve singlehanded.

Total efficiency is an absolute, and striving for it in teaching is a form of the Jehovah-complex—the teacher as almighty creator. In this spirit it is often proposed that every teacher should adopt some program of social reform and inculcate it along with arithmetic or history: another kind of false leading. For then the tangled issue of academic freedom[7] comes into play and fritters away energy, while the teacher splits his loyalty between the urge to teach his subject and the duty of drilling and catechizing for the new order. Once for all, teachers have neither the time nor the means of refashioning our children's souls one by one or our entire culture *en bloc*.

Of Human Freedom

With regard to what is taught, the mistake of progressive education is to believe, or to affect to believe, that learning can be entirely divested of drudgery. Rousseau, who is the spiritual father of modern progressive education, made no such mistake. He pointed out in the *Émile* that although many things can be rendered more attractive than they usually are, only a desire to reach a certain goal drives the student on through inevitable drudgery. When the goal is seen by the teacher but not by the learner, the drudgery has to be enforced by the more farsighted of the two.

Reading and writing can be taught more easily in some ways than in others, but that they should be taught and taught early admits of no question. The same applies to other rudiments. The justification for cramming them down, if no other way offers, is that the present pain is kinder to the child than the humiliation or sense of failure later on. These are the pupil's basic "needs."

What these needs are in college is not so easily determined. A college degree is supposed to stand for a minimum proficiency in studies, but no agreement exists about what these studies are or how proficiency is to be measured. The progressive colleges differ from other kinds only in having a broader curriculum and in teaching as a regular subject the practice of the fine arts. Whatever be the method, the progressive college must give its students the chance of finding out what the world of educated people think, talk, and write about. Personality is worth nurturing, but it exists only in a world of objects and persons, which are many and various. A whole personality is better than a fragmentary one, but it cannot be nursed in an intellectual vacuum.

The fact that every year in this country progressive institutions graduate several hundred students of both sexes who have acquired not only knowledge, but also confidence and poise, sufficiently answers the accusation

150

that these schools are mere playgrounds or country clubs where young people do everything but get an education. If these colleges do educate, however, it is because the students have been for four years under the care, not of doctors and psychologists, nor even of "educators," but of teachers—men and women whose interest is in the life of the mind fully as much as in the life of the young. These teachers have doubtless thought much about the difficulties and the ways of teaching, but they know that their first duty is to teach. They agree with Shaw that "those who can, do; those who can't, teach"; only they expand the aphorism to read: "Those who can teach, do; those who can't, become educators."

4

While the errors of progressive education range from amateur psychiatry to noneducation, those of studying only the classics range from useless smattering to empty formalism. The humanities curriculum proposes that certain great books will be understood in their general as well as their particular meanings. The truly educated man will not merely quote aptly in the drawing room, he will have made the thought of Aristotle or Spinoza a part of his being and an instrument of his own speculation. He will have had varied emotional and intellectual experiences and acquired a greater power of receiving and communicating ideas.

It is pleasant to look back upon the days when Latin was the universal language of scholars and every educated man had his classics—the common classics—at his fingertips. But a glance at the social and political world of that day does not favor the hope that Unity follows the classics the way the Constitution follows the flag. In all things "interpretation" leads to diversity rather than unity. The Catholic Church knew this and discouraged the laity

from reading the Bible.[8] The Protestants did not, and
their sects multiplied instead of uniting on the basis of the
Sacred Book. Some comprehensive system must accom-
pany Bibles or classics, and it is no accident that the University of Chicago, which took the lead in advocating
the return to the humanities, is also the institution where
Aristotelianism and Neo-Thomism found their most
urgent expounders.

This link between general education and a metaphysical system was made clear by the then President Hutchins, who quoted Saint Thomas on the same page as he described the medieval unity and its "orderly progression
from truth to truth."[9] But this unity is doubtful as a historical fact, and dubious as an aim. The disputations and
excommunications of the medieval universities form a
unity only when we think of the words and texts argued
about, not when we look at the purposes involved.
Medieval opinions diverged all the way from pantheism
to rationalism and from mysticism to materialism, very
much as ours do. Looking at our own intellectual scene
from outside would give an equally unified picture, for
we all haggle over the same points and rehash the same
authorities. Yet as living witnesses we feel "chaos" because small differences matter. Only the future historian
will see them merge into one grand harmony that he calls
the Spirit of the Age.

One can therefore agree with President Hutchins's
vigorous attack on the false practicality of American colleges and the bastard forms of vocational training given
there under the name of education, without feeling impelled to strive for an intellectual order of the kind he
describes. That order is bound to be an orthodoxy and
the chief trouble with an orthodoxy is precisely that it is
not order but a constant strain in the direction of the
rigid and final. Disputation and excommunication are its
devices; but disputation is not discussion and excom-

munication is, on the face of it, lack of communication. Orthodoxy is the antithesis of a living and variegated culture; it is undemocratic at the very root of democracy, which is the individual mind.

This is not the place to examine the ultimate value of Aristotelianism, but to notice its salient characteristics of definition, division, abstraction, and classification—in a word, its architectonic qualities. Though symmetry is a form of beauty and suggests stability, it may at first sight seem odd that a system of this sort should excite the American undergraduate imagination.

Yet for a good many years some of the most intelligent students in our universities have been caught by the charm and have worked to become Aristotelians.[10] They indoctrinate themselves through books, periodicals, and personal friendships. As one of them put it in self-deprecation, it ranks almost as a game: "Subject, Object—who's got the Essence?" The appeal is not surprising. System—and that is the strength of fascism and communism also—fills two very great emotional needs of the young. It provides certainty, in more or less close alliance with religious emotion; and it offers a method enabling the learner to stretch out his slender stock of knowledge. In a world of ceaseless upheaval, the essences and categories of Aristotle and Thomas stay put. In a world where things are seldom what they seem, the practice of logical definition and deduction is a reassuring routine.

Like progressive education, the metaphysical approach to the liberal arts makes use of a special vocabulary—this time truly scholastic—which often satisfies the user in proportion as it mystifies the listener. Essence, category, proportion, substance, ratio, existence, form—these are the ready-made containers for the stuff of life and art. The aim is to deduce particular truths from axioms and definitions and so to approximate mathematical, that is to say absolute, truth.

Of Human Freedom

Insofar as it values precise thinking this attitude is admirable, but insofar as it disregards the variety of fact and feeling, it is an intellectual and practical menace. An example will enable the reader to judge for himself. What follows is taken from the University of Chicago Syllabus for the introductory course on the History and Appreciation of Music, and though excerpts are to a certain extent unfair apart from musical examples, the characteristic language suggests the spirit behind the teaching:—

> *On Melody:* Melody is a succession of tones in proportion, having a beginning, a middle, and an end. But musical proportion differs in some respect from other proportions. . . . Consequently it is false to think of a proportion as the equality of any two relations or ratios. Between any two terms there are usually more than one relation. What the proportion states is the *equivalence of one kind of relation.* . . . Generalizing . . . we may say that *any four terms are in proportion by virtue of two equivalent relations.* An understanding of melody requires an understanding of proportions of tones.[11] [Italics are in the original.]

Whether or not this is the best way to teach the appreciation of music, the finality of each statement raises an even graver question: Has music anything to do with this particular way of "approaching" it? No indication is given that it is *a* view and not *the* view to have upon music; that this was not Haydn's or Beethoven's view; and that perhaps there is no single view which will encompass every kind of music. The method cannot allow such an idea, for as its favorite adjective tells us, it is "fundamental." It gladly smothers the medley of history for an abstract unity. The fact that, like any method, it can be used well or ill hardly alters its relation to culture and contemporary society. With regard to both it seeks

154

to transcend experience and to substitute for the difficulties of tangled fact the single difficulty of verbaliza-
tion. That in so doing it solves the riddles of the empirical
historian of art is apparent, but how satisfactory the solution will prove is another question. It gives a fixed rule
to test things by, like Marxism and fascism, but unlike
them it prepares as yet no revolution. It offers a change
only in setting up new cultural standards different from
those of the liberal-scientific tradition.

5

Elsewhere than at Chicago and St. John's, American
education has swung back to the classics: an excellent
move, but it must not be deemed a panacea. Like other
subject matters, the classics produce no ideal student,
guarantee nothing. That is why the temptation will be
strong to smuggle in a system along with the books. The
system will offer to harmonize three thousand years of
great literature and draw the lesson of history in favor of
Saint Thomas or Aristotle or Karl Marx. But that attempt itself will generate a counterblast to sweep the
classics out again. The theory which the classics do not
in fact support will be combated in the name of some
other absolute good, and the classics will be relegated
once more to the back shelf in favor of a "modern" education.

Yet the classics, taken simply and soberly, illustrate an
important, modern, democratic ideal—that of diversity.
They unite only on a few moral precepts which form the
wisdom of the ages upon the good life, self-control and
self-respect, and the primacy of mind and soul over gross
self-seeking. Apart from this ethical cargo, and also their
power as works of art, the immense value of the classics
is that they show the many purposes and occasions which
the indomitable energy of free mind has seized upon and

turned to use. The sense of continuity through chaos, the fellowship of genius across time and space, imprint themselves on the receptive mind, however modern, and give it strength—the strength of tradition, which without this possession is an empty word.

But the classics alone cannot fully educate. Modern man needs a knowledge of science and social science, and the practice of the arts as well. To leave out the first two is like leaving theology and politics out of Dante. It is to try to educate a man into a mere slice of himself, split off from his own time and his own place. As for the practice of art—a notable contribution of Progressive Education to the curriculum—it affords the surest way of teaching the rebelliousness of matter, the love of patient application, and the indefinable worth that intelligence confers on mechanical skill. It is or can be the gateway to esthetics, which is the pragmatism of the artist.

With respect to pedagogy—its second contribution— progressivism has made us face the fact that children are individuals, in body and in mind, and that they cannot be educated by mass methods. The learner's motives, powers, and difficulties have been studied by the progressives and often overstressed, but we are not likely to forget the lesson by which the school has been turned from a polite jail to a nursery of minds. What we are likely to forget is that the "best method" and the "best curriculum" do not exist and therefore cannot insure the "best results."[12] These imaginary absolutes are fatal, particularly if the teacher is constantly thinking of the method or fiddling with the curriculum. Devotion to ideas and to minds on the part of the teacher is the only practical method, and the whole range of past and modern culture, including science and the arts, is the only defensible curriculum. For the sake of vividness these subjects had better be learned from what Chesterton called "rambling through authentic books and countrysides." Hence the value of the humanities when free from system. No one can learn everything he needs to know in four years of college, and hence must learn how to learn in his own way. For reminding us of this truth, the progressives deserve our thanks. Beyond this lies not theory but classwork.

Habits of thinking and comparison, of concentration and curiosity, the repression of intellectual fear and intellectual egotism, the desire to gauge particulars, be they books or men, in their own terms and not by rote or by signs—these are the individual guarantees against absolutism which a modern curriculum in a democratic school can instill. The rest is and will remain self-education. Once out of the teacher's hands, man and society are responsible for the culture they create in common. The social goals, the political principles, the utopian hopes that the adult democrat will entertain, will undoubtedly be moulded to a certain extent by what he has learned in school. But these are most often furnished by other minds, original geniuses who are happily uneducated or differently educated from the mass. Consequently, after having traced cultural democracy to its source in the individual mind, then to its first nurse, the school, I must now on the home stretch follow it back into the arena of social aims and political struggles from which we started.

11 *The Mirage of Utopia Unlimited*

ALL tinkering with education implies that the school controls the future, and in times of adversity everybody is a passionate futurist. That is why in all ages the use of the school for reforming the world has beén advocated as a matter of course. Plato suggested it; the Church grew by it; Locke and everybody else since has urged it, the while making a lunge toward the school system ready to hand. The nineteenth-century liberals and nationalists worked the device for their ends; the twentieth-century dictators are amazingly successful. The odd thing is that although it is possible to make young children believe in complicated ideas about the flag, the Trinity, and the moral benefits of wholesale assassination, it seems utterly impossible to go against the current of habit and establish once for all such things as Christianity, democracy, tolerance, and a desire for peace.

The reason may be that the teachers are tainted and transmit their spiritual disease just as parents transmit their neuroses to their offspring. Cut off a whole generation from its poisoned predecessors and it would still have to be taught somehow—by books or television—which would introduce the germ of the sinful present and make the birth of the new society anything but the immaculate conception which is desired.

The illusion is to believe of the world that it stays put and that it can change. We want to stamp on our children a fresh pattern that will stick and make the world forever better; we fail to see that if this were possible, our present pattern would stick first and make change impossible. This is the snag in every mechanical determinism—Neo-Marxist, racial, or scientific—which I have combated in this book.

The truth seems to lie altogether away from these contradictory hopes. Things change in detail through the action of mind. Things stay the same if the lump stays unleavened. Matter falls back and crushes us; mind makes itself a little room. That mind brings about changes within itself is not an illusion. Psychoanalysis proves it daily. Intelligence is intelligence because it is not a machine. The stimulus to its action is sometimes external—hard fact, moral suffering, temptation; sometimes internal—what we call a "mere" idea. But the idea has to be impelled by a common emotion. The kind of intelligence demanded here implies this harnessing of common emotions to workable ideas, for it is clear that no mechanical method enthrones democracy, fascism, or any other utopia permanently and automatically. To expect it is to expect perpetual motion in physics. For if mind in the fullest adaptive sense is not made the agency of change, we are left with the one-sided absolutes which abstract thought invents—Race, Material Cause, Historical Fatality—and these betray in their flaws their bookish origins. The government of the world is in any case a dynamic and personal thing. A man should sometimes refrain from saying, "I live in a democracy," and say instead: "I experienced democracy last Tuesday afternoon." His good fortune is not a uniform condition of life but a temporary equilibrium of forces.

In the face of this reality, one of the strangest facts in history is the indomitable belief of man in the possibility of good government. The myth of a Golden Age, the Garden of Eden, the Republics of Plato, Thomas More, and Karl Marx, bear witness to their anger at the mismanagement of human affairs and their hope of a more lovable future society. History records no utopia and carries no hints that good government is possible.[1] Nevertheless men have not really doubted this particular possibility even though they have almost invariably doubted the possibility of flying or of laying a cable across the Atlantic Ocean. It seems a kind of animal faith.

In the contemporary world, where so many utopias, tried and untried, compete for attention, it is almost indecent to speculate about the wellsprings of hope. The more pressing task is to determine what are the chances of a better life and what the risks of achieving it amount to. For on one point all proposers of new schemes agree, namely that one cannot make an omelet without breaking eggs. And the proverb must be translated by "breaking heads."

For the happiness to come we must not only destroy, maim, kill, and imprison; we must do it under conditions which rule out care and justice. Heedless damage and death must be dealt out, not for fun, but for eternal peace. It is then not a low or cowardly calculation to try to measure present ills against future good: it is the question at issue. When the Paris Communards burned the Hôtel de Ville in 1871—from real or fancied necessity, not from wantonness—they destroyed among other things some paintings by Delacroix. What are paintings to the happiness of thousands? Nothing, of course. No man with a spark of humanity would hesitate to burn down whole museums to *insure* the happiness of a single family. But we have not fully answered our question: were thousands made happy by the destruction of the Hôtel de Ville? The answer is again, No. But they might have been; nothing in this life is certain. We cannot let uncertainty stop us. True. But is it not equally true that we go on, generation after generation, killing and burning for our ideals, not (as we pretend) in vain hope but actually in dull despair? What is our warrant for thinking that violence will bring peace; for being so sure that our spasmodic efforts do not accumulate net losses of life, health, and civilization; for hoping that we shall some day cash in net gains of happiness and good government?

2

Good government, like happiness, requires no definition: it is whatever the petitioner desires. His judgment is final. If we wish to find out whether history has ever seen a good government we have only to look for peoples or periods that have never uttered complaint or known unrest. But since it would be casuistical to take quiescence for acquiescence, the test must include a judgment of past conditions from our point of view. If we should now consider them inhuman and intolerable, the government, however stable, was not good. Search as we will, we find no trace of any people anywhere at any time that fits this requirement. Voltaire did say that happy peoples had no history, but that was only his way of saying that history mentions no happy peoples.

It might be argued that the two centuries of peace under the Caesars were just what we are looking for. The eager searcher is struck by the unbelievably protracted peace in those two centuries. But that peace must be examined: there were raids on the borders of the Empire; revolt, murder, and stern policing within. If we admit that war is no part of good government because it is always an evil to someone, then whether the war is a national war, a colonial war, a civil war, or even repression for law and order, it is still a form of violence which must lower our opinion of the government in proportion to our estimate of the total well-being.

In putting it as naïvely as this, one is open to the rebuttal that "man being what he is," every government is compelled to use force at some time on somebody. What the practical man wants is a government using the least amount of force compatible with stability. Just so; and since that maxim is the fundamental maxim of all the governments that have ever existed, the conclusion follows that good government, define it as you will, invariably becomes actual government, that is to say, bad government.

Accepting this conclusion is a beginning of wisdom, or at least of knowledge: government uses violence because it is of the essence of good government to maintain itself, from which it follows that there is and can be only one kind of government. Faith in utopia believes that there can be different kinds of government. Politicians, historians, philosophers—everyone speaks of monarchies, aristocracies, republics, despotisms, as if the names stood for structures differing from one another *toto caelo*. Yet it should seem more instructive to recognize the historical generality that to date there has been on this earth only one kind of government, to wit, oligarchy, or the rule of the few.

By one kind of government I mean here one species, one sort, not necessarily one *form* identical in every detail. In detail no two governments are alike, as no two men are alike. Even our common names, democracy, monarchy, and so forth, never imply that all democracies are alike, or that the American democracy has remained the same from its beginnings. I contend only that in their functions, methods, and difficulties, all governments that we know anything about have been oligarchies. The oligarchs have not necessarily been of one class, rank, race, or fortune. They have been *de facto* groups wielding actual power, whether they had right or reason, sense or selfishness.

One knows nothing about a government as a living act if one looks only at the written or traditional constitution under which it operates. The historian's task is to find out which wheels and levers move and by what power. The central fact in government is that every regime has a façade and the governing is what goes on behind it.[2] The façade is nothing but the difference between our individual and our social selves objectified. We do not behave in public as we do in private. The difference is our façade. It took Swift's wonderful eye to imagine a parliament of naked men, and on reflection the vision stands for as remote a utopia as that where the philosophers would be kings.

We are wrong to think of the façade as hypocrisy, or as the peculiar wickedness of the group in power. Everyone at times finds a façade convenient and calls it, without hypocrisy, "preserving reputation" or "maintaining prestige." The government is the *res republica,* the Public Thing, which means that its chief strength is its prestige. Without prestige, it must exert force to govern at all. With prestige in the form of rules, traditions, and the mere show of force it can maintain itself, which is its prime duty; and this in turn is why it can keep going best in its own ruts. Faith in forms keeps a nation united in times of stress, and the same faith in prestige guides diplomacy and makes for war. Material greed itself makes use of that general trust and could not act without it.

Within the nation it is the façade that makes corruption necessary and possible; for the façade must have a human embodiment—a bureaucracy (meaning by the term all the agents of government in any system), and this bureaucracy makes for stability and corruption. It is stable because the rules in any government are of necessity few and stiff compared to the myriad situations of life; and it is corrupt because corruption is the short cut taken to make things work. As Mirabeau put it, *administrer, c'est gouverner; gouverner, c'est régner; tout se réduit à cela.*

The obvious suggestion is, why not get rid of the bureaucracy and substitute for it a government of active, intelligent, unhampered men? This is the plausible appeal of dictatorship, whatever its label or doctrine, but the futility of the scheme is apparent. First, the transition is painful, like all transitions, and second, the government of bright young men soon becomes a new bureaucracy that behaves exactly like the old, from the same necessity. In government, the difference to look for is not whether a man is wearing a white shirt or a black one, but whether he is in front of a desk or behind it.

If these are constant facts, what we change when we get tired of our bureaucracy and have a revolution is the decoration of the façade. We had a king, we have a president; we had notables or peers and now have senators and deputies. *Plus ça change, plus c'est la même chose,*[3] except in one important respect. The actual living persons in the comedy do change with changes in the façade. One day Metternich rules the domains of the Hapsburgs; the next day he is hiding in a laundry cart bound for London. One group triumphs while the other goes into exile. For most people that is victory enough. We are refreshed by seeing new names in the new chapter of history and we infer from it that the problem of government has gone one step further towards solution.

Gazing at the mirage, we confound our private feelings with what we have heard about political evolution towards this or that goal. We rejoice at the liberation of the serfs by Alexander II because freeing serfs is a Good Thing. We scarcely pause to inquire whether they were better off, whether they liked it, whether their owners liked it. We do not much care about the owners because we feel that furthering the interests of our friends is furthering the interests of good government. We are also swayed by a tacit assumption of racial responsibility, whereby if a Russian nobleman has been brutal to his serfs, it marks an evolutionary advance when the serfs massacre his son.

Until one has seen through this fiction of large-scale evolution and class continuity one cheerfully accepts the succession of revolutions and reactions as proofs of progress. Yet even to the uncritical reader it must be a mystery how the bourgeoisie, for instance, goes on century after century "rising to power." The middle class, we are told, "emerges" in the towns of the twelfth century. It seeks power in England and France at every turn during the next six hundred years. It "really governs" under Henry VII, Richelieu, and Louis XIV. It is still rising and demanding and governing before, during, and after the French Revolution. The years 1830, 1832, 1848, mark dates in the history of its climb, and still in our midst the bourgeoisie is represented as both having and seeking power. The whole account is true, but it is intelligible only if we visualize successive generations of men of varying origins, fortunes, and purposes striving to possess a portion of oligarchical power in the form that it takes in their day—becoming judges by purchase in old France, marrying into the aristocracy in England, grasping industrial power in modern states, or passing the Mandarin examination in the China of yesterday.

3

Grant that oligarchy is a constant fact; is it not restricted or enlarged, worsened or mitigated, by the particular shape and temper of each government? It undoubtedly is, but in lesser degree and in different ways than we commonly think. Forgetting evolution for the moment, we must ask: Was the power of the Persian despots, for example, any more arbitrary than that wielded by a modern state? Let us remember the illusion of the façade and the fact that we tend to compare the *palace* histories of the past with the *national* histories of the present. Modern ways of ruling seem to us more congenial, perhaps because they are our own. No one says "Off with his head" in blank verse, but anarchists are executed, a troublesome witness is found dead, pinned on a main-line railway track,* undesirables are deported, labor agitators are gassed or jailed for life, with thorough efficiency. The Oriental despots were not, as we seem to think, always reclining on couches, but were busy and harried men surrounded by a host of lesser despots, whose task was to keep the masses quiet and at work, or else patriotic and at war. Their methods were simple: Violence and Cajolery—changeless in essence, although we have multiplied their means and forms.[4]

Since democracy remains an ideal that moves us strongly, we are bound to ask whether in all the Mismanaged Past there was not a truly self-governing body, directly so or by representation. The smallest conceivable city-state or the most compact New England town meeting fails to meet the question affirmatively. No private institution so meets it. Executive power is always vested in a few to carry out the wishes of the temporarily gathered many. Who are these few? Persons of influence, position, wealth, prestige—one or all of these, or else their paid agents.

Approach the question from the other side: what despot that we know of has ever ruled singlehanded? Is it even conceivable that a man who had not a great many willing supporters should stay in any place of power for a single instant? We are naïve about Louis XIV when we think he said, *"L'état, c'est moi."* One has no need to read the *Mémoires* of Saint-Simon to realize that *l'état* was a host of persons, many in an absolute sense, though few relatively to the population of France. When we find a prince without ministers, advisers, courtiers, mistresses, father-

* In France after the Stavisky scandal (1934).

confessors, physicians, relatives, and soothsayers, it will be time to talk of absolute monarchs.

The Asiatic or the fascist system of despotism can no more avoid the common rule than the rest of mankind. Whether Janizaries, Praetorian Guard, Brown Shirts, or Party Members, some compact body of followers must exist in whom power is centred and through whom it filters down to a larger group of consenting subjects. Rulers and immediate followers together form the oligarchy that exerts violence in order to maintain themselves in power when cajolery has worn thin. Abdul-Hamid II was as much the absolute sultan of Turkey as Huey Long was master of Louisiana, but not a whit more, and the duration of their sway is no sure indication of their individual skill at a game where chance is a greater factor than any statesman is willing to admit.*

With modern dictators it is of course difficult to say how far the oligarchy extends and whence the power really springs, but the difficulty of a measurement is not a denial of the thing to be measured. The demagogic dictatorship of Pericles in Athens; the bureaucracy and the army in the Later Roman Empire; the 140 Whig families behind Parliament in the eighteenth century; shifting groups of bankers and manufacturers in the modern nations—these are some of the oligarchies that have assumed the running of governments behind the façades, regardless of the style of the pillars drawn up by theoretical draftsmen or described by stay-at-home travelers.

The oligarchy that constitutes the actual government is a shifting and ill-defined body of men. Some drop out and others join the ranks. In normal times, habit and

* It is always irritating to read in histories that this or that ruler averted disaster by "wise moderation" or, just as often, by "quick and stern repression." The historian always knows how the crisis turned out, but never why, any more than the statesman who took the step or the poor student who is made to learn the conclusion.

momentum keep government going despite irregular conflicts within. In periods of civil or foreign war changes are more visible, but change is incessant. Napoleon could have died a first lieutenant and George Washington been hanged as a rebel: the accident of persons and names does not alter the institutional character of oligarchy, and an idle king belongs to it much less than a base-born major-domo who really rules.

To particular persons, obviously, the façade which results from shifts above and pushes from below can make a great difference. When the Russian oligarchy consists of landed proprietors, it is comfortable to own land; but when a similar oligarchy with a similar foreign policy and a similar idea of crushing dissent happens to be made up of proletarians, then it is the part of wisdom—or the lucky privilege of birth—to belong to the proletariat, or rather to that part of it that forms the oligarchy. The history or alleged evolution of governments is then the revolving kaleidoscope of chances whereby certain groups and individuals find themselves within the circle of power. Preference for one form of oligarchy rather than another can therefore be only a relative preference. It must rest on a modest estimate of human powers and probabilities. It cannot be an absolute utopian preference, as for light after darkness.

4

What is the explanation of this iron ring that prevents essential change? If one is convinced that "human nature" is not evil and fixed, but is neutral and plastic, one finds here a tantalizing mystery. Man may be an artist in the midst of nature, he is anything but a political animal.

A possible answer lies in the properties of number. The difficulty of coördinating individual acts, even when the wills are at one, is the reef on which we split. Any theatrical or musical rehearsal, any picnic or committee meeting, shows us for what we are. It is not because we are human but because we are individuals that we fail. The doctrine of individualism in politics and economics may have accentuated our sense of singleness, it did not create it. Consciousness of self, the strict privacy of all experience, is an irreducible fact. The impossibility of any large group governing itself is matched by the impossibility of any system creating a spontaneous union of wills, an obstacle that does not even take into account the further one of the masses' indifference to the task of government.

Somebody—in the end an oligarchy—must use propaganda and coercion to achieve the minimum of concerted effort we are familiar with. This minimum is always threatened by war, riot, and crime; so when the governors say that to protect themselves is also to protect the mass, they are stating a verifiable fact. Periods when one grand oligarchy has replaced another have been times of panic and self-perpetuating violence. The religious wars of sixteenth-century France, the Thirty Years' War in Germany, the Civil Wars in England, do not make attractive reading to civilized beings. It is precisely to prevent such interregnums, that in so-called quiet times the oligarchy finds itself waging a ruthless and constant civil war.

This permanent war is bound to be unjust, costly, and cruel. It keeps opposition alive through generation after generation of the governed. So unbreakable is the chain that oligarchies violently set up with an altruistic purpose seldom get the chance to govern well, owing to the necessity of governing *now*. Stalin can do no better than Cromwell because he must quell rebellion, still every appetite, before he can give up killing and empty the fortress of Saint Peter and Saint Paul. In order to *pacify* and *appease,* Cromwell and Stalin must shoot down and imprison. Government is thus always doing in some measure the opposite of what it seeks to do. It must insure the good life in order to maintain itself, and to do this it must take away the life of those who challenge it.

Since Karl Marx it has become a commonplace that if the perennial difficulty were considered not as a problem of government but as one of economic organization, automatic forces would come into play and settle the trouble. With plentiful goods equitably distributed there would be no dissenters, no raging appetites, no strikes, no treason, no civil war. Marx foretold in sober terms a peaceful passage from the dictatorship of the proletariat to blissful anarchy; while other anarchists, seeing the prospect with as much clarity as impatience, have at once set about making bombs.

Unfortunately, this economic machinery and this method for disposing of our present rulers alike suppose the very thing that is in question. One can even grant the questionable point that all conflicts would cease with the satisfaction of bodily wants and still ask how that satisfaction could be insured without oligarchical, that is political, administration. Administration means rules, decrees, paper justice; and behind it, a fallible human oligarchy committed to enforcement like any other. Government does not occur only at the capital or the county seat; it occurs wherever someone is in charge of someone else or controls some desirable good. This need not discourage us in the attempt to reach economic equality, but it should make clear what the achievement of that particular desire can and cannot do for us. It will feed and clothe us, a mighty boon, but more than that we must not expect.

Socialist songs usually have a refrain that begins, "To-morrow . . ." To-morrow, even with socialism, we shall have to do what we must do to-day—constantly repair and refurbish our government. To-day or to-morrow government must roughly satisfy all sides before it can deserve the epithet "good" in the sense of tolerable. We are not to become "impartial" or "dispassionate," but we must test in our souls whether we really accept the rough side of whatever we propose. Too often in contemporary programs of reform and revolution one notes a fatal transition from the ideal Good-of-all to Good-of-people-like-me-and-my-friends. It is a very natural substitution: charity begins at home and Plato wanted the philosophers to be kings. But let us at least know what it is we are proposing and for whom it is intended. Those who expect that their particular utopia will support not only life, but also civilization—science, the arts, the life of mind—must not hope that any automatic process will do this. Many a plan begins: "Those who show talent will be educated at public expense; young talent will be rewarded and facilitated. . . ." But what talent? Who will test it? Examinations, boards, juries—fallible men very like those we know, biased by individual experience and, though *possibly* free from economic interest, just as passionately at odds over prestige, persons, ideas, techniques, and philosophies.

The generous sentiment that forgets these realities contains the seeds of present danger. If we start with material things, one step after another leads us on. Our utopia is reasonable, possible, within our grasp. It is all but done and only the ignorance and folly of our enemies keep us from reaching it. No wonder we think those scarcely human who reject what Plato planned and Christ died for! The selfish man attached to his poor present must be sacrificed, the last obstacle laid low, regardless of the apparent loss. It is only temporary: the dead bodies, the gutted buildings, the burnt books, will be replaced by new, fresh, glorious ones. Even the shattered men who have done the task of "social sanitation" will pass and be forgotten in the endless peace to come.

When we awaken from this dream we must confess

that we have been rationalizing our wild desires in the teeth of stubborn fact. We have been fascinated by an absolute. Good government, happiness, culture—one and indivisible. Our intuition may be sound. But because these may be conceived of as one does not mean that it can be won at a single stroke by doing something violent and decisive. Coercion and cajolery in government we cannot do without. They must be mitigated, like pain, counterbalanced by practical justice, relieved by social and economic equality if we can achieve it. But let us not believe that magnifying Force and Folly will magically turn them into saviors which will disburden us of our responsibilities.

In a dictatorship of any kind, liberal or reactionary, the oligarchy will still be on top of most of us; and its atmosphere will be even more coercive and nonsensical than that under which we live, because it will be new. Democracy considered as the special atmosphere of a perennial oligarchy is not better than fascism or communism in an absolute sense. It is better only for those who prefer pluralism and the fruits of culture to unanimity and the security of regimentation. Democracy tends to preserve the diversity of nature. It is not a high-pressure machine geared to a single task that requires the whole people to live in the dictator's "atmosphere of high ideal tension."[5] It is not a uniform pattern, which is why it permits and demands a ceaseless variety of achievements, local but genuine, temporary but valuable. To the outside observer Democracy looks imperfect and inefficient; to the insider, its defects show it to be not essentially different from other governments, *as government*. But as a culture, and when that culture is actively kneaded by critics and creators, it affords more air to breathe freely, more room to move in, more variety to encourage further variety.

Hitler is therefore right when he says that democracy tends toward anarchy: that is the main point in democracy's favor. His error consists in thinking that democratic anarchy is necessarily unbearable, that it exists everywhere at once, and that it grows endlessly. It obviously does not, any more than fascist or communist uniformity controls every moment and portion of life. And that being so, it is the futile attempt to control, followed by failure and by ever more desperate violence, that makes the totalitarian atmosphere unbearable and destructive. On this point the life histories of past oligarchies and the spectacle of present-day strivings toward utopia must be thrown into the scales on the side of democracy. Uniformity is more of a myth than anarchy is an evil.

The democrat and the reformer had better frankly face these alternatives and continue the struggle here and now in something like sober despair. No man is compelled to be cheerful against the evidence of his senses, however driven he may be to better his lot. But he loses more than he gains by disregarding his limits. This seeming despair is only active resignation. It carries with it no danger that mankind will lie down or history suddenly come to a standstill. The danger is that wild, unreconciled despair, coming after exorbitant hope, will inspire the creed of action for its own sake. No one grieves because he cannot dig through the Rockies with his bare hands. The barriers nature imposes we circumvent rather than break down. We do not wildly swing from thought to action and back to thought. We try to think as we act. Life in society presents the same unyielding obstacles which crush those that run into them full tilt. Their example may make us pause and admire a reckless courage, but unfortunately for the world, the principle of heedlessness remains oddly at variance with the pragmatic method of science and of art, which are so far the only notable successes in human affairs.

12 *Democracy: Pragma versus Dogma*

"WHAT has been concluded that we might conclude about it?" asked William James towards the end of his life. James's implied warning is not amiss for any author who comes to his last chapter. The temptation is strong to tie up the threads of discourse into a bowknot which may increase for the reader the value of the package he has bought. But the fondness for conclusions is part of that fondness for absolutes, for systems, which has been the target, not the goal, of our discussion. Every criticism and suggestion in these pages has urged that we deal individually with particulars, judge the thing itself, shape it to our purpose, and resist being diverted by formulas. The consistency of this advice is itself a formula, but it is, or ought to be, a flexible one. The unity it offers is the unity of many-sidedness which belongs to a democratic culture and constitutes the democratic atmosphere.

At the same time, the critiques offered here have an immediate application. They are addressed to those concerned with American culture in its fourfold division of art, science, education, and government. What the reader chooses to think or do in other realms, in his capacity of taxpayer or church warden, is his own business. The pragmatic and historical attitude behind these chapters can indeed be carried over into many activities, but there again the formula will need adaptation by taking thought. All things have links with other things, but men are not all of a piece, which may be a reason why programs of total action seldom lead to action at all, but only to signing pledges and attending meetings. Except for economic or professional groups, which are organized for stated ends, the channels of disinterested action in the daily democracy of life remain unorganizable.

This is not to draw a moral contrast between interested and disinterested action—both are legitimate—but to distinguish pragmatically between the self-regarding emotions and the desire of intelligent men to "do something" about the world. Even when doing good, with no hope of reward, sane men want to be practical. What then is practical? Whatever achieves its aim, without costing more than it is worth in energy, freedom, or self-respect. It is practical to give money for the defense of political prisoners and organize the University in Exile; it is unpractical to waste one's time denouncing the French novelist Romains as a fascist or excommunicating one another over minutiae of doctrine. It is unpractical to inveigh against progressive education or psychoanalysis on the slight knowledge that hearsay affords. It is practical to keep an eye on the school one's children attend and the methods one's associates habitually employ in any profession. Power depends on knowing situations concretely; that is, power should be exerted against undemocratic opinion or behavior in circles where our person or our intelligence can make a difference. An ounce of overt pressure on the point is worth a pound of confused indignation and bluster. And if the temptation occurs to act indirectly, by blackmail or bribery, the tempted may be assured that they will so soon find themselves at the mercy of their own tactics that all talk of democracy by them or anybody else will become irrelevant.

So much for individual action. My concern here has been with culture. In a certain sense my speculations form an autobiographical report upon the opinions of my neighbors in the professional and educated world. It is

175

their views and prejudices, their unstable despair or faith in democratic conduct, that affect my life as the corresponding thoughts in me affect theirs. Whatever limitations my survey has had, its lessons, rightly or wrongly drawn, can be indefinitely extended and reshaped to particular purposes.* The possibility of democratic conduct, I have tried to show, is primarily a cultural affair, and only indirectly one of government. Democracy is a philosophy and it has had its native philosopher. I refer to historical-minded Pragmatism and to William James,[1] whose thought has animated all of my strictures and sustained my faith through the contemporary chaos. "Real culture," as he finely said, "lives by sympathies and admirations, not by dislikes and disdains." And on another occasion: "You can give humanistic value to almost anything by teaching it historically. Geology, economics, mechanics, are humanities when taught with reference to the successive achievements of the geniuses to which these sciences owe their being. Not taught thus literature remains grammar, art a catalogue, history a list of dates,

* In his *Autobiography*, G. K. Chesterton gives a good example of the way in which the test of practicality can be mistaken, because it requires more intelligence to carry out than the ordinary man of affairs is willing to exert. The village where Chesterton lived decided to put up a war memorial in the form of a cross. Some citizens objected to the symbol because of its popish associations and suggested the building of a clubhouse for discharged veterans. This proposal was at once felt to be more "practical" than a "useless" cross. But the cost of the clubhouse, the admission or exclusion of the veterans' wives, the question of site and suitability, soon created such vast problems for the small community, and split it into so many parties, that the alleged practicality not only vanished, but entirely overshadowed the original idea on which all were agreed—namely, to put up a war memorial. Chesterton concludes: "If they did not approve of wasting money on a War Memorial, let us scrap the War Memorial and save the money. But to do something totally different from that which we wanted, on pretense of doing something else which we did not do, was unworthy of *Homo sapiens*. . . . I got some converts to my view; but I think many still thought I was not practical; though in fact I was very specially practical, for those who really understand what is meant by a Pragma." (P. 240)

and natural science a sheet of formulas and weights and measures."[2]

These two attitudes give a clue to the principle of my search. The mechanical, the formulated, the materialistic, the abstract, the rigid—all that I have called for short the absolute—have seemed to me stultifying ways of interpreting life and reality. When I considered how interpretations tend to usurp the place of the things they interpret, the use of those categories appeared to me as a gangrene in the culture that harbors them. And wherever I saw mischief or menace in the present world, I believed I saw the symptoms leading me back to some form of absolutist or materialistic thought.

It remained for me to substantiate the surmise. I tried to show first how a democracy depends on cultural means for its maintenance and I met the charge of decadence by pointing out how political standards, whether fascist or revolutionary, dry up the life of culture through regimented art. Turning then to the problem of social art for a democratic society, I examined the persistent confusion between the art that pays and the art that lives, and suggested that the latter can be produced and financed only if those who pretend to prize it are free from the lesser absolutes of snobbery, nationalism, and preciosity. Society at large must allow as much variety in art as in life, the interplay between the two producing that criticism which is essential to both. This raised the issue whether art is real or illusory and by extension, what in life was real and what was neurotic or abnormal. The test of reality turned out to be social and democratic, normality having no other meaning than "that which is accepted by the social group as useful."

A misinterpretation of psychoanalysis, which is invoked in the charge of "escapism," proved to be the link between the current understanding of man's mind and the art or science he produces; and since man also pretends

177

to be a political animal, his behavior in society as a rational being or as a self-styled activist must be dealt with at the same time. Human freedom was then seen to arise from the normal working of the mind in grappling with difficulty. Absolutism is but an attempt to solidify a single result, one happy thought, into a universal rule. The modern superstition of race exemplifies this process to perfection. It pretends to explain by refined discrimination; it ends by discriminating nothing and destroying everything. It seeks the clue to culture and presents us with the mystery of matter working miracles by itself.

Since one of the motives to race-thinking is to achieve scientific exactness, and since for many people science and materialism are identical, I next took up scientific method, social science, and certain pseudo-sciences in order to disentangle the scientist's pragmatic method from the absolutist ways of his imitators. Outside natural science the historical method emerged as a valid instrument of research. The results of that research must, however, be diffused if they are to influence conduct. A brief excursion into the nature of propaganda and the use of words followed as a corollary, and since the evils of propaganda depend on our receptivity, the intellectual weapons that schooling provides had to be tested. The chaos in education is fortunately clearing up, but its ordering must not be doctrinaire. A rounded education beyond common literacy can be given in the eight years of high school and college, which should equip democrats for their many tasks. Thereafter individual talent and social wisdom work out their mingled destiny. On his part, the individual must forgo the absolutist hope of the perfect state: it is a mirage that neither history, nor practicality, nor the just expenditure of life warrants. In pursuing that will o' the wisp, democratic man overlooks the tasks near at hand whose performance can make, locally and temporarily, for the good life.

Throughout this argument two ways of thought were used: historical and pragmatic. The first is self-explanatory. The second demands a few words more. Pragmatism is a test of truth which states that *that is true which works.* Truth has no other meaning, but beware of taking "works" in a childish or stupid or cynical sense. The theory that the moon is made of green cheese undoubtedly *works* up to a certain point. It is true insofar as it accounts for the observed coloring of the moon on recent nights. But it "works" no farther. To-night the moon is red—is it a Dutch cheese? The inconsistency is disturbing: the hypothesis must be revised. The truth will be found when all the facts man is capable of observing have been taken into account. When men are able to predict eclipses, tides, phases, and a thousand other phenomena which they desire to understand, they have reached a pragmatic truth. To it must be added the vision or truth of the poet, painter, and musician, for these record the inner feelings, fluid perceptions, and other discoveries which art embodies in tangible forms. Science without art is joyless, and art without science misleads. The two together constitute our truth so far, a man-made truth about "real" things, which are what man *troweth* about the elusive Experience that only he works upon, through the genius of great men and of society.

The notion often attributed to pragmatic philosophers, that an idea is true if it succeeds in fooling a number of people, is no more a representation of pragmatism than green cheese is a quarried chunk of the moon. It is a caricature of the very subtle doctrine which teaches that any idea, however true it seems or has seemed, is never final or absolute. It is continually subject to revision in the light of the consequences it leads to—actual and logical. Every idea is compelled to meet the requirements —material, moral, or esthetic—of the inquiry. Far from being a doctrine of self-deception, Pragmatism wars against self-deception by putting the weight of human pride behind consistency of ends and results rather than consistency of means and formulas. It forces outcome to match pretensions and it does not accept substitutes, verbal or sentimental, for the fulfillment of human desires. It is vigilantly aware that there are more ways than one of conceiving and reaching desired ends, and it is not satisfied until some kind of provision has been made for those things or purposes that any single system leaves out.

That pragmatism in action is intellectual democracy preserving and extending itself is not hard to see.[3] Whenever democratic culture produces a new idea or institution, the value of that institution or idea must be tested by comparing its proposed goal with its actual effects. Culture is man-made and man-destroyed. No fatalism produces or safeguards it. Men of culture must therefore make it their business to defend it. This of course assumes that our society wishes to foster its characteristic culture and remain democratic. It is possible to maintain that other things come first—that economic security or political unanimity is infinitely more desirable. Pragmatism allows even those views, if their advocates explicitly accept the consequences; but it disallows the pretense that burning books or making musicians scrub floors is really the *true* way of fostering art and encouraging freedom. The pragmatic thinker is also willing to suspend meditation and go into action upon a given plan, but he suspects that a violent repudiation of thought and a plunge into activism with one's eyes shut will not bring about the millennium. This plunge does not promise empirical satisfactions and this therapy of contraries has only a kind of surprise plausibility. Its appeal to the "long run," a long run that never ends, is adjudged an historical and logical fallacy in a world where culture is perishable and life short.

Since shortsighted stopgaps are obviously unpractical,

pragmatism needs and uses history. By its means the long run is a verifiable measure stretching back into the past and suggesting judgments applicable here and now. The very weakness of history, its uncertainty and inability to put things into neat bundles, is its great advantage over ready-made systems. Its difficulties force the student's gaze to discern in each event and person its unique character, to mark and remember its own shape. It is a discipline that strengthens individual judgment and keeps bright the points that connect imagination with present reality.

History, one may say, is a bookish thing that takes leisure and special training. Alas! Nothing is simple. Few things are easy. Does the mere doer's contact with the present suffice? What is the present but an ambiguous sentence out of its context, a human embryo in the fish-like stage? We confess it in all our fact-finding surveys. Our government is more and more a research bureau. We want a broader base for thought and we need, clearly, a wider inquiry than can be made by interrogating the living. Interrogating the past through history implies no fatalism, nor its modern avatar—mechanistic evolution. The past does not freeze the future; but it often shows that the happy idea we are about to carry out has already been tried with negative results. We may try it again, often we must, and it is then useful to know where and how it betrayed mankind before.

The lesson of history is not that there is no lesson of history, as Hegel thought, but that there is only one: Many men, many minds. Hence tolerance—or mutual annihilation. Our attitude towards our opponents suffers from forgetting it; or rather, it is we who suffer. We may enjoy ascribing folly to them *a priori,* but it hurts them less than it hurts our own idea. Rage may win physical combats; in the battle of ideas it does not so much strengthen as stiffen our minds. It begins the distortion and perversion of our idea itself. The prophets and teachers of humanity have been flexible and abundant minds; their disciples dry and narrow systematizers. It is the latter who repeatedly fail. Something indeed they put through, or put over, but it is something so different from what was originally wanted by anybody that the success wears a constrained look. It is absolutism in the place of pragmatism, the perilous victory that soon or late breeds revolt.

In realms where consequences are less immediate than in politics and moral conduct, the pragmatic historical attitude attends particularly to the nuances of concepts. Pragmatism is conceptualism, or the philosophy of image-making mind, as opposed to absolute mechanisms of all kinds. It believes that ideas are at best stiff though useful ways of crystallizing the flow of experience. It uses them precisely as we use words to deal with things. Words, ideas, conventions—these rigidities are as indispensable to the life of society as to the life of culture, but they become falsehoods and stumblingblocks as soon as it is forgotten that they are abstractions. If instead of revising and altering them constantly to fit what we perceive we fall down and worship them, or put our pride and prestige in defending them, we lost sight of our purpose in our devotion to faulty means. We become in the technical sense fanatics—persons who "redouble their energy when they have forgotten their aim."

Whether it be the scientific method or progressive education, or psychoanalysis or the use of certain words —to trust these valued means in situations where they do not fit, or which they no longer fit, is worse than having no means and taking no action. For the system fails to do what we want to do, at the same time as we stamp upon life a pattern alien to our own desires. The Bed of Procrustes is the true original of such a scheme and its inventor was the Arch Neurotic, forever baffled by the unsatisfactory proportions of his victims. Its opposite, the true success of art, depends upon the genius for abandoning a successful system as soon as it ceases to work.

It follows from all this that no one idea, no one explanation, is omnicompetent. Contradiction, or at least nonuniformity, is a fact of experience. Even in the world of matter, physicists have found it expedient to regard light now as waves, now as corpuscles, for it acts by turns as if it were each of these things. Men in society act in more diverse ways than matter, and the arts are pragmatic techniques for recording these diversities. Whether it is the art of governing by laws or of causing laughter by animated cartoons, it is a pragmatic business. The hope that we can reduce each art to a simple set of rules and be done with thinking about it forever after is not merely illusory; it is to any conscious mind a repulsive idea. The apparent, or even the real, hopelessness of, as we say, solving difficulties by taking thought should not make us despair. It should make us continue to think, to think better, and, testing the thought, to act. As Meredith sang:—

> More brain, O Lord, more brain or we shall mar
> Utterly this fair garden we might win.

If there is reason and experience and the satisfaction of desire in this view, there cannot be the slightest doubt that civilization presupposes democracy. Despite its errors and perversions, indeed because of them, democracy guarantees two conditions of continuing thought— a certain popular indifference and a strong discouragement of cocksureness. In democracy the two go in inverse ratio, and between them grows tolerance. Demos is dangerous, Demos is fascist, only when the indifferent are cocksure and the thoughtful have ceased to care.

In a democracy the great problem is less to educate everyone beyond his intelligence than to make the intelligent socially responsible. To think and act socially is not a kind of charity to one's neighbors. It is a form of self-preservation. Nor need it become a crusade, but only the fulfillment of individual capacities. The best scheme is no better than the brains of those who carry it out, and it is surely ruined by those who think that faith is the only equipment needed to make it work. Mere intellect is dry and sterile, but mere devotion can turn the myriad small good things of life to dust, especially if it is boundless in its scope and starts reform on a planetary scale. The quest for certainty, the passion for absolutes, and, even worse, the lustful desire to enforce the commonest jerry-built absolutes are the death of democratic culture and a denial that life is worth living.

If the desire to accept rather than to exclude, the love of variety rather than of sameness, should combine with an actively pragmatic attitude in a democracy like ours, even the private, static absolutes in philosophy or religion could find a place.[4] The man who has at last got hold of THE truth can live among the infidels if his intelligence is as strong as his faith. Let him take out his conviction in superiority and pity, if he wishes; let us huddle together along creedy lines whenever tolerance or faith falters; and let us indulge our moods of optimism and depression, remembering that they are moods; but in the name of peace and pragmatism, let us face with open eyes a pluralistic world in which there are no universal churches, no single remedy for all diseases, no one way to teach or write or sing, no magic diet that will make everyone healthy and happy, no world poets and no chosen races cut to one pattern or virtue, but only the wretched and wonderfully diversified human race which can live and build and leave cultural traces of its passage in a world that was apparently not fashioned for the purpose.

Notes and Acknowledgments*

The references given below furnish support for the positions taken in this book and also serve to indicate my indebtedness for facts and ideas.

Besides these obligations, I owe gratitude to a number of friends and colleagues whose opinions on contemporary affairs have either sharpened by opposition or confirmed my views. I cite with pleasure: Dr. John Adams Abbott, Cuthbert Daniel, Clifton Fadiman, Dudley Fitts, James Gutmann, Moses Hadas, C. J. H. Hayes, Barbara Jones, the late Nicholas Kaltchas, Helen Merrell Lynd, Barbara Spofford Morgan, Charlotte Muret, Dr. Wilmoth Osborne, Wendell Taylor, and Fredrika Tuttle. In addition, the entire text has had the benefit of Lionel Trilling's careful criticism, for which I cannot adequately thank him.

For permission to reprint copyright material, grateful acknowledgment is here made to the *American Scholar;* the Association of American Colleges; Chapman & Hall, Ltd.; Constable, Ltd.; The Critics' Group; Faber & Faber, Ltd.; Harcourt, Brace & Co.; Harper & Brothers; the *Herald-Tribune Books;* Alfred A. Knopf; Little, Brown & Co.; Longmans, Green & Co.; The Macmillan Company; Methuen, Ltd.; the *Nation; The New Statesman and Nation;* W. W. Norton & Co.; Bernard Shaw; Sheed and Ward; *Social Studies;* William Troy; the University of Chicago Press; and H. G. Wells.

* Written in 1937 and 1938, these notes often refer the reader to periodicals and books of the Thirties. I have not tried, twenty-five years later, to find parallels or substitutes for the illustrations that seemed to me apposite then, even though in the chapters themselves I have replaced old names and old cases with fresher ones.

185

Notes and Acknowledgments

EPIGRAPHS

Byron's declaration of war against the enemies of Thought is from *Don Juan*, Canto IX, Stanza 24. The passage from Henry Adams refers to the heroine of his satirical novel, *Democracy* (p. 342), published anonymously in 1880 and never publicly acknowledged by him. (But see Henry Holt's article in the *Unpartizan Review* for January–March, 1921.) The sentence from Mill concludes his *Essay on Liberty,* and the bit of friendly chaffing between William James and Josiah Royce is reported in the former's *Letters,* Vol. II, p. 135.

CHAPTER 1

1. Note in the *Nation* for February 18, 1939, the *political* expectations of a supposedly *cultural* organization:—

The Leftist League of American Writers once held a meeting to discuss the adverse treatment of leftist books by reviewers on capitalist journals. George Seldes and Max Lerner were the speakers. But the invitation to Lerner didn't make clear the point of the meeting. After Seldes had related instances of the mistreatment accorded his book on the press, Lerner caused some embarrassment by declaring that his own experience was just the reverse. He said the "unfairest" review of his book had appeared in the *Daily Worker* and added that one of the few publications which had thus far failed to review it was the *New Masses*.

CHAPTER 2

1. In a review of a book by Harold Laski, Ernest Sutherland Bates said:—

The struggle for liberty happens to have antedated the rise of capitalism by some two thousand years. Mr. Laski writes of liberalism as if Socrates and Jesus, Wyclif and Huss, had never existed. His neglect of the dim beginnings of the Parliamentary system in Magna Carta and the Barons' War violates the principle of historical continuity. The Bill of Rights of 1689 meant something more than the triumph of capitalism, and the Reform Bill of 1832 was more than an unimportant capitalist concession. The "ruling class" of which he writes is an abstraction, and the line between power and no power, clear in logic, is always obscure in practice. [*Herald-Tribune Books,* Jan. 15, 1939.]

2. It is one thing to condone international anarchy, out of cynicism or indifference, and quite another to know what to expect under its regime. In an article on Spain, Professor Salvemini felt bound to explain to his readers that "in the operation of an alliance a twofold conflict takes place: one outside the alliance, between the allied powers and their common foes; the other within the alliance, between the allied powers themselves, in that each tries to prevent its ally from becoming so strong that it will no longer need an ally. A good diplomat always expects his best friend of today to become his worst enemy of to-morrow, and conducts himself accordingly." (*Nation,* Feb. 18, 1939.) This truth may be deplored, but the danger of being astonished and morally aroused at each fresh instance of it is graver than we imagine. Besides being wasteful, the emotion is weakening, for it satisfies purely egotistical feelings and makes them masquerade as altruism. It is the righteousness of Mrs. Jellyby, who neglected her children and wept for the plight of the natives of Borrioboola-gha.

3. The history of Greece, where democracy first flourished, gives us the example of the rise of the "tyrannis." They rose to power by becoming the champions of an oppressed class, and when once in power tried to abolish the old aristocracy in favor of a sort of classless state where equality served as a substitute for liberty. When the tyrants fell they were replaced, not by old or new aristocrats, but by *nouveaux riches.* In other words, the three oligarchical rules were, in order: aristocratic, democratic, and plutocratic. (See E. M. Walker, *Encyc. Brit.,* 14th ed., Vol. X, p. 767.)

4. The contrast of Hume and Johnson is suggestive. The latter hated and fought the former's skepticism, as did all "right-thinking" people in the eighteenth century. Nevertheless Hume, in spite of his friends' fears and his enemies' hatred, was able to live in comfort, hold public posts, and publish at will. At the same time, though Johnson was a pillar of Church and State, he kept and used extraordinary freedom in speech and thought. Thus the aristocracy that allowed Hume and Johnson to coexist and work freely was tempered by cultural democracy.

5. From this view of democracy it follows that wherever we find a spontaneous cultural product that we value—be it a book or a painting, the Mermaid Tavern or the Literary Club—we can say there was to that extent an island of free democracy. That radical, Kit Marlowe, whom Mrs. Hallie Flanagan had to identify for the Dies Committee, seems to have been killed because in his circle Elizabethan democracy failed: a friend or enemy turned informer against him and the bugbear of atheism was used to make the law an accomplice to murder. These probabilities are typical. One thinks of Blake's situation during the French Revolution or that of German-American intellectuals during the First World War.

6. Compare Burke, *Thoughts on French Affairs* (Everyman ed., p. 290): "... The interest in opinions (merely as opinions and without any experimental reference to their effects) when once they take strong hold of the mind become the most operative of all interests, and indeed very often supersede every other."

7. It may serve as a kind of reassurance to remember that in 1902 H. G. Wells foretold the life history of democracy with fair accuracy and apparent equanimity:—

So armed, the new democracy will blunder into war, and the next great war will be the catastrophic breakdown of the formal armies, shame and disasters, and a disorder of conflict between more or less equally matched masses of stupefied, scared, and infuriated people. . . .

Now, foreseeing this possibility, it is easy to step into the trap of the Napoleonic precedent . . . with the pressure of coming war, or in the hour of defeat, there will arise the man. He will be strong in action, epigrammatic in manner, personally handsome, and continually victorious. He will sweep aside parliaments and demagogues, carry the nation to glory, reconstruct it as an empire, and hold it together by circulating his profile and organizing further successes. He will . . . codify everything, rejuvenate the papacy, or, at any rate, galvanize Christianity, organize learning in meek, intriguing academies of little men, and prescribe a wonderful educational system. The grateful nations will once more deify a lucky and aggressive egotism. . . . [*Anticipations,* Harpers, 1902, pp. 185–186.]

8. This book not being a work of metaphysics, the meaning of Absolutism, Mind, Matter, and Materialism varies in the context. To make a show of strict definition, as is the fashion nowadays, only to find it impossible to imitate mathematics, is to impose on oneself and one's readers. Similarly, it would be a distraction and not a help to fight out in the main body of the text the old problem of Mind and Matter. To the philosophical student it will be clear that the declared indebtedness to James—and, it may be added here, to Berkeley—puts the writer among those who reject subjectivism equally with material causation. Objects are real, they truly exist, but the forms of their existence depend on mind. A myth, a legend, or a superstition has a kind of existence, distinguishable from that of objects, though equally real in its effects, as everybody allows. The realm of mind is thus continuous with that of being and its values are to be judged by nothing else than human minds. What mind is, in itself, cannot be answered except metaphorically. Since it means existence, it can be called God, or the Life Force, or Energy, according to one's religious, poetic, or scientific bent, without enlightening us much further. As usual, the important thing to decide is what mind *does,* not what it *is.* (See also Note 1 to Chapter 12.)

CHAPTER 3

1. See below Henry Adams's view quoted on pp. 193–194.

2. Hitler's speech, *Deutsche Allgemeine Zeitung,* Sept. 8, 1937, p. 3.

3. The first exhibition under this name opened in Munich, city of museums, in 1937. A second, in July 1938, elicited further art criticism from the People's Chancellor, who indiscriminately called all modernists "cultural Neanderthalers." (*N. Y. Times,* July 19, 1938.) The phrase is somewhat inconsistent with the decadence theory: anything more fresh, robust, or with finer prospects for the future than Neanderthal Man it would be hard to find.

4. *Deutsche Allgemeine Zeitung,* Sept. 10, 1936, p. 1.

5. See T. S. Eliot's Preface to the *Essays for Lancelot Andrewes,* p. ix; John Strachey's *Coming Struggle for Power,* Chs. X and XI; Lenin's opinions, quoted in Max Eastman's *Artists in Uniform,*

pp. 217–252; the Russians' attitude, in N. Slonimsky's *Music since 1900*, pp. 402–403, 549–555; and Hitler's numerous charges in his annual Culture Day speeches at Nürnberg.

6. Cubism and Futurism date from 1905–1912; Schönberg's *Harmonielehre* is dated 1911; Stravinsky's great music, and the Russian ballet which it was written for, were first produced in 1910–1913; the sculpture of Archipenko, Brancusi, and Duchamp-Villon was exhibited in Paris before 1914; the Imagists, Simultanists, and Unanimists published their first technical essays in the new poetry between 1907 and 1912; Perret's daring use of reenforced concrete for wide spans and vaults was first shown in the St. Malo Casino in 1900, and though other features of modern architecture had been tried in America and Germany for ten years before, the new style established itself after the turn of the century. In the dance, Mary Wigman was creating her first independent composition—a *Hexentanz* without music—in the late autumn of 1913 in Munich, at the time that the theory and technique of her teacher, Laban, were gaining renown. Finally, two important practical arts were achieving success in the same decade: the art of flying and the art of the cinema.

7. At the first exhibition of Impressionists, in a period of post-war depression and alleged decadence, namely in 1874, there were over one hundred painters represented. Now we remember half a dozen masters.

8. In the mouths of antimodernists, this seems to mean sensuous, crass, appealing through texture and color rather than line and design. In attacking materialism I am not concerned with matter or substance in the vulgar (and acceptable) sense of the term, for it is precisely the business of the artist to use matter, materials, common or uncommon stuff. All the arts do so. The dancer uses her body and the musician sets material air and eardrums in motion by means of material instruments. (For another refutation of the same charge by an expert, see Walter Gropius, *The New Architecture and the Bauhaus*, p. 79.)

9. Hitler called the monuments of culture "the altars on which mankind recognizes its higher missions and feels its worthiness." (Speech on Culture, Sept. 1933, p. 18.) General Franco proclaims that "with reference to culture and style, we have established the Institute of Spain, with the reorganization of the Royal Acade-

mies. . . ." (Speech at Saragossa, April 19, 1938; Mussolini's and the Russians' official stimulation of art is too well known to be detailed.)

10. The old Symbolist cant used to be, "It's pretty, but is it art?" indicating the absence of idea in much popular art. Now the same query, "Is it art?" refers to the opposite—unpopular art—and means, "Such ugliness must be intentional—there's too much in it that I cannot understand and not enough satisfaction for the senses." (See *N. Y. Times Magazine,* March 8, 1936, especially the excellent conclusion by A. H. Barr, Jr., p. 23.)

CHAPTER 4

1. Quoted in Eastman, *Artists in Uniform* (Alfred A. Knopf), p. 135.

2. Motto of the John Reed Club.

3. See, e.g., *The New Masses,* late spring of 1935, *passim,* and Note 5 to Chapter 3.

Prokoviev, on Soviet Music: Documents; trans. by Alexandra Groth, American-Russian Institute Publication, Hollywood, 1948.

4. In *Pravda* for Jan. 28, 1936, an officially inspired article condemned the opera *Lady Macbeth of Mzensk* as "deliberately anti-melodic and subservient to 'Western modernism.' " The argument was the old commonplace: "To follow this 'music' is difficult; to get anything out of it, impossible. . . ." And further: "Does not the fact that this opera is messy and absolutely devoid of political connotations contribute to its success among the bourgeoisie, that it tickles the perverted tastes of its bourgeois audiences with its fidgeting, screaming, neurasthenic music?" (N. Slonimsky, *Music since 1900,* W. W. Norton, pp. 402–403.)

5. The fiction crops up everywhere: in Bertrand Russell's *Sceptical Essays,* pp. 114–115; in F. L. Lucas, *Life and Letters,* Nov. 1931, p. 325; in the Report of the 1935 Writer's Congress, *New Masses* for May 7 of that year, p. 21.

The facts which refute this theory can be found in Wordsworth's own memorandum in Christopher Wordsworth's *Memoirs,* 1851, 2 vols., Ch. II, and in Crane Brinton's admirable volume on the *Political Ideas of the English Romanticists,* 1926, pp. 54–59. (See also D. W. Rannie's *Wordsworth and His Circle,* p. 90.)

Mr. Brinton points out that Wordsworth and Coleridge did not change suddenly, but gradually gave up the too artificially acquired catch-phrases of rationalism and liberalism. The poems where Wordsworth repudiated the revolution, because he found it "as bellicose and unjust as the old monarchy had been," are great poetry precisely because the indignation and patriotism in them are natural and not pumped out of doctrine into verse. Moreover, as late as 1809, Wordsworth refers to the Napoleonic system as "the child of noble parents—Liberty and Philanthropic Love." (Brinton, p. 58.) The "before and after" theory is too simple. Professor Garrod believes that the Coleridge friendship accounts for the changed quality of Wordsworth's verse.

6. *Décade, 30 messidor an* III.

7. His ability to furnish this sort of theatrical fare was coupled, naturally enough, with the ability to turn his coat as often as required. He began as a royal flatterer (*Contes aux Enfants de France*), was known during the Revolution as the most competent craftsman for the stage, trimmed his sails to succeeding political puffs, and died at the age of seventy-nine in 1842, having worked *faithfully* for six different and incompatible regimes.

8. *Moniteur,* October 1793, *passim.*

9. See the latter's *Memoirs,* Ch. XXIX.

10. Mr. Percy Scholes's book on *The Puritans and Music in England and New England* reënforces the point made here about the Puritans' fondness for art. Music, dancing, and the publication of French novels continued in England under the Commonwealth and Protectorate. If we forget the clichés about the "Puritan mind," the question is left open why there was no great creation in an age as well supplied as any other with appreciators of art. (See also H. W. Schneider, *The Puritan Mind,* Ch. III.) The now accepted theory about *Pilgrim's Progress* is that Bunyan wrote it, not during his first twelve years' imprisonment, but during a later and shorter spell in jail, in 1675.

11. *Clarke Papers,* Camden Society, 1891, Vol. I, pp. 325–326. (See also pp. 238, 277, 301.)

12. Max Eastman's *Artists in Uniform* deals with some aspects of the Russian theory and practice of art control. It contains also a valuable translation of Polonski's *Outline of the Literary Movement of the Revolutionary Epoch,* pp. 217–252. (See pp. 43 and

note, 135, 226–228, 230–231, 243.) Trotzky, Bukharin, and Frunze have also written about literature under communism, supporting the position of Marx, Engels, and Lenin. (See also Edmund Wilson in the *Atlantic Monthly* for Dec. 1937.) Compare this uniform front with Oscar Wilde's great essay on *The Soul of Man under Socialism,* especially the passage: "The spectator is not the arbiter of the work of art. He is one who is admitted to contemplate the work of art, and if the work be fine, to forget in its contemplation all the egotism that mars him—the egotism of his ignorance, or the egotism of his information." (*Essays,* p. 45.)

13. *On Shakespeare* (Smirnov and others):

The conclusion that Shakespeare was the ideologist of the bourgeoisie is inescapable. It is impossible, however, to designate him as such without reservations. The rapacity, greed, cruelty, egoism, and philistinism so typical of the English bourgeoisie—embodied in Shylock, Malvolio, Iago—are no less scathingly denounced. His strong sense of concrete reality deterred him from creating a utopia, yet he possessed utopian ideals. At a later stage of bourgeois development, Shakespeare became a threat to that class which had given him birth. The *bourgeoisie have never been able to understand or accept the revolutionary elements in Shakespeare's work,* because these immeasurably transcend the narrow confines of bourgeois thought. And so, the bourgeoisie have crowned him with the empty title: "The Universal Man." [*Shakespeare, a Marxist Interpretation (The Critics' Group),* 92–93.]

Mr. Smirnov has an excellent insight into character, a keen sense of literary values, and a most winning way of writing. These accentuate the forced character of his Marxist "interpretation," which would be so much truer to Shapespeare and to Marx if it took up its subject for the sake of social history and not in a spirit of systematic hindsight.

CHAPTER 5

1. "Democracy is an infinite mass of conflicting minds and of conflicting interests which . . . becomes resolved into . . . a vapor, which loses in collective intellectual energy in proportion to the

perfection of its expansion." (*Degradation of the Democratic Dogma*, Preface by Brooks Adams, pp. 108–109.)

2. *Ancient art.* See Thucydides and Plutarch, Rostovzeff, E. M. Walker, and Ferdinand Lot. Compare Bliss Perry, *Heart of Emerson's Journal*, pp. 25, 104, for Emerson's complaint about the forced patriotism of his day which produced only feeble works.

3. A letter from the treasurer of an important American orchestra speaks of "the unequaled opportunity of forty-six continuous weeks of employment" for the musicians at an expense of $600,000, of which only $510,000 is covered by ticket sales. Gifts and endowment must pay for the $90,000 deficit. Arrears in taxes on the concert hall, mortgages, and other expenses are met by "generous gifts," bequests, and the Annual Appeal, from which these facts (also annual) are quoted.

4. Perhaps the clearest statement of the difference between a work of art for connoisseurs and one for ordinary consumers is Max Eastman's small volume *Journalism versus Art,* published in 1916 But see also Bernard Shaw's *The Sanity of Art* for another sense of "journalism," a sense in which, as Shaw proves, all great art is journalism.

5. This may seem an undemocratic notion; actually, it is not an opinion but a fact, readily ascertainable from a consideration of our most democratic form of "good" literature—the best seller. A book such as Margaret Mitchell's *Gone with the Wind* had sold, by the end of its first half year, 894,000 copies. Whatever its further circulation may be, it was even at that time an extraordinary publishers' success. The population of the United States at the same date was 130,000,000. Multiply the sales of the book by five readers and subtract from the population two fifths for children and others physically unable to read the book, and the ratio of readers to non-readers remains roughly one to twenty. If Fuller was right in saying that "learning has gained most by those books on which the printers have lost most," the so-called spread of culture among a modern enlightened population can be estimated at its true measure.

Mr. Edward Weeks, in his useful and entertaining book, *This Trade of Writing*, gives figures on the great American best sellers. The list is naturally disappointing "as literature," but it is still more disappointing as a proof that not even *Freckles* or *David*

194

Harum reached a majority of the contemporary American people. Mr. Weeks points out that in the publishers' peak year, 1929, roughly 84,000,000 copies of books were sold. If we disregard the actual duplications resulting from library, school, and other purchases, and generously assume the democratic principle of "one man-one book," the figure still leaves 46,000,000 bookless people in the United States, a public which, one hopes, is catered for by magazines, but which it would be idle to regard as panting for "the best that has been said and thought in the world." (See also R. L. Duffus, *Books and Their Place in a Democracy.*)

The unnatural effort of reading is and will remain a limiting factor, so let us look at the more easily grasped art of the theatre. Mrs. Hallie Flanagan, who made the Federal Theatre Project a reality, reported than in the "tenth month of its existence" it employed "12,464 people, 50 per cent of whom are actors. This army of theatre workers operates 153 producing theatres located in 28 states . . . and plays to an aggregate audience of 350,000 people weekly. . . . Statistical surveys show that the majority, not only of these audiences, but of those who pay the low admission fee of ten to fifty-five cents, are people who have never seen a play." (*Magazine of Art Reprint for Federal Theatre,* Jan. 1937, pp. 5–6.)

When the movies were at their peak, the weekly attendance in the United States was 130,000,000, and there were at that time over 20,000,000 radio-receiving sets in use. The comparison of these figures gives us an idea of the important numerical difference more or less accurately related to a cultural one. This difference, it must be repeated, carries with it no moral or other blame; and we can applaud Mr. Mortimer Adler's plea in behalf of the movies as art without forgetting that Hollywood's version of *Vanity Fair* and Thackeray's are two distinct things having little more than a basic plot in common.

6. In *Wealth and Culture,* Eduard C. Lindeman published in 1936 a valuable survey of one of the forms of modern art patronage, the Foundation-Grant system. After interpreting his results, Dr. Lindeman added the following conclusion:—

In a society . . . in which private profits had been entirely eliminated, or in a society in which the state itself claimed the right to acquire surplus wealth either through taxation or direct expropriations, there would still exist a definite cultural problem which would need to be attended to by governmental or private agencies. The above statement may, of course, be contested: there are those who believe that economic security is in itself a guaranty of automatic cultural development; that truth, right, good and beauty combine to form a lively cultural ferment the moment the basic economic problem is solved.

Dr. Lindeman believes this "naïve belief" rests on a lack of discrimination between the "efficiency and collectivism of civilization" and the "sufficiency and freedom of culture." (P. 61.)

7. The preface of almost any serious biography will prove my point. In nine cases out of ten the author speaks of "the prolonged misunderstanding" or the "unjust detraction" which his subject has had to endure. The book itself generally quotes the depreciatory remarks of opponents, and Lord Morley used to refer to "defective and traditional criticism" as the explanation of so much anarchy of opinion. Two recent examples of the need for "rehabilitation" can be cited: Carl Grabo's study of Shelley, *The Magic Plant;* and Quintana's *The Mind and Art of Jonathan Swift.*

Books like Wilbur C. Abbot's *Adventures in Reputation,* 1935, give a truer sense of the ups and downs of critical "dissensus" than the ordinary textbook or one-sided biography, while a study of opinion on a single man such as *German Opinion of Gustave Flaubert from 1857 to 1930,* by E. E. Freienmuth von Helms, reveals the chameleonic appearance of a great artist when seen through two or three dozen critical minds.

8. In his survey, *College Music* (Macmillan), the American composer Randall Thompson reports the kind of dry stuffing that so often passes for the "historical approach." Here are notes on the genre, from a college lecture:—

"With the establishment of the University of Paris, a school of music was considered as important as any other department. The Netherlands School (1425–1625); the Gallo-Belgic School (1360–1460), Before this time you've had your Crusades; your Mongol invasions; your Genghis Khan. Mohammedanism introduced. Papacy at Avignon. Milan Cathedral begun 1346; Petrarca, 1304–1374; Boccaccio, 1313–1375. . . . Obrecht, the teacher of Erasmus." Asked class who Erasmus was. None spoke. Explained that he was "the man who introduced Humanism into England." [Pp. 227–228.]

196

This cultural performance, of which only a fraction is reproduced here, contained twenty-six proper names, ninteen dates, and fifteen technical terms. It was read by the teacher from beginning to end, within the usual class period of fifty minutes.

CHAPTER 6

1. Eddington, *The Nature of the Physical World*, N. Y., 1928, p.283.

2. In *The Neurotic Personality of Our Time* (N.Y., 1937, pp. 14 ff.) Dr. Horney points out both that culture must be taken into account before deciding what is neurotic, and that Freud culpably neglects this element of judgment. Otto Rank, in his *Wahrheit und Wirklichkeit* (Leipzig, 1929), makes the same criticism and shows that a neurosis, far from being an "imagining," is on the contrary a loss of the normal power of imagination. (Pp. 7–15; 41–55.) See also Ferenczi, "Stages in the Development of the Sense of Reality," in Van Teslaar's *Outline of Psychoanalysis*, p. 108.

3. Horney, *op. cit.*, pp. 22–29.

4. In *The Criterion* for July 1933, p. 553.

5. For those who are conversant with Freud's doctrines, two further points should be made, both dealing with "Escape."

Says Freud: "Art is almost always harmless and beneficent; it does not seek to be anything else but illusion . . . it never dares to make any attacks on reality." (*New Introductory Lectures*, Norton, page 219.) And in his critique of the German novel *Gradiva* (in *Delusion and Dream*), no less than in his famous study of Leonardo, Freud passes from the artistically or biographically "real" to the imagined, dreamed, or remembered, as if they were on an identical plane. What Freud evidently assumes is that, just as in sleep there is a turning away from the reality of the outer world (*Lect.*, p. 27) and at the same time a continuing concern with the reality of our wishes which makes for dreams, so in art there is the same kind of dream symbolism (pp. 39–40) and *therefore*—here comes the fallacy—there must be in art a turning away from the reality of the outer world. A good analogy between art and *dreaming* has led him to a false one between art and *sleeping*. But the difference between a work of art and a dream is precisely this, that the work of art *leads us back to the outer reality by taking*

197

account of it. Art is thus equally "true" with science when properly understood. A scientific formula has to be interpreted and so must a fable, and both are real and true where they are meant to apply.

The second point is related to the one just made and confirms it. Freud again and again uses legend and anthropology to establish the "reality" of his hypotheses. He says, for example, "We have found a remarkable reference to this correlation [between ambition and urethral eroticism] in the legend that Alexander the Great was born on the same night that a certain Herostratus, from a craving for notoriety, set fire to the famous temple of Artemis at Ephesus. It seems the ancients were well aware of the connection involved." (P. 140.) What Freud is really saying is that *ancient* art and legend can disclose truth by taking account of reality, whereas other art is a "harmless illusion."

So far from this "connection being well-known to the ancients," it is mentioned in only three major writers—Valerius Maximus, Strabo, and Plutarch—and the latter calls it a "frigid conceit" invented by one Hegesias. In other words, it is a piece of artistry, the factual truth of which is unprovable. The psychoanalytic truth rests on Hegesias's having had a shrewd insight, expressed in symbolic language. Freud is therefore probably right in his ulterior analytic purpose, but the more he is right psychoanalytically, the more he is wrong critically in his estimate of art.

6. *New Intro. Lect.,* p. 240. Freud mentions James in the *Autobiographical Study* reprinted at the end of the volume, *The Problem of Lay-Analysis* (Brentano), 1927, but although that reference is an admiring one it is personal and has nothing to do with James's ideas. James on the contrary mentions Freud (*Varieties of Religious Experience,* p. 233) with a clear sense of the implications of Freud's early work, and he elsewhere insists in a philosophical way on some of the main points of Freud's general psychology. These were, as a matter of fact, in the air, and a careful reader of Schopenhauer, Stendhal, Butler, and Nietzsche could have gone a long way towards anticipating Freudian conclusions about art and life. The immense value of Freud is that his clinical work gives a striking confirmation of what is in truth a philosophy generated in the nineteenth century. That is why it is such a pity to see him misapply his own results to the broader issues which also interest

Notes and Acknowledgments

him—religion, anthropology, art, and society. But one should not require a great man to be free of all superstitions. Newton, we must remember, was an alchemist, and Kepler an astrologer.

CHAPTER 7

1. This sample of race thinking is from the N. Y. Philharmonic Society program (*not* the Program Notes) for Friday, January 7, 1938. See also a more plausible form of the same reasoning in an article by Mr. James Travis on "Celtic Elements in Beethoven's Seventh Symphony," *Musical Quarterly*, 1935, p. 255.

2. In *Deutsche Allgemeine Zeitung*, Sept. 10, 1936, pp. 1–2.

3. The definition is by the elder Huxley, quoted by Jevons in his *Elementary Lessons in Logic*, p. 283.

4. The enlightened scholarly works of Albert Guérard, from *French Civilization in the 19th Century* (1914) to *Literature and Society* (1935) are devoted in part to the elucidation of this tangle of race. His conclusions anticipate what I say here.

5. The chaotic terminology is not confined to the so-called scholarship of the subject. It exists in the popular mind as well. The 182 persons competing for an Essay Prize offered by an historical society in 1938 all put down "American" after the word *Nationality* which appeared on the identification blanks. But these same persons put down after the Word *Race* a wide range of terms indicative of (1) color (e.g., White, Negro); (2) nationality (Russian, German); (3) language (Hebrew, Aryan, Teutonic); (4) subnationality (Scotch, Irish); (5) anthropology (Nordic, Indo-European); and (6) geography (Caucasian, Malayan). Had these answers been tabulated, would the German-American, for instance, have admitted belonging to the same race as his fellow competitors calling themselves Nordic, Teutonic, and Indo-European? If so, would he not also have been White and Caucasian, and perhaps Aryan? What concrete things do these overlapping and indefinite words point to, beyond the individual's knowledge that his parents were born in Germany, that he is tall and rather blond, that by a pleasant fiction his leather-colored exterior is called white, and that he has chanced to learn one set of race words rather than another?

6. The "author" is the now forgotten dramatist Buirette de Belloy. (*Œuvres Complètes*, 1779.)

199

7. Berlioz was born in the southeast of France, at La Côte-St.-André, not far from Grenoble. His ancestry was local for two centuries before his birth, in a region once closely allied with Italy, and earlier with the Roman Empire. The writers who want to tie him to some racial tree do violence not only to the probabilities of an untimely "mixed" ancestry, but also to the facts (e.g. the gratuitous "Gascon" theory) and to Berlioz's mind as well, for he was a natural cosmopolite, equally at home everywhere in Europe, provided he was with artists and cultivated men.

8. Stalin's *Report on the New Constitution,* 1936, p. 8, says that 80 to 90 per cent of Soviet intelligence comes from the working class. This assertion is so far a mild form of race-thinking, assuming as it does the existence of a natural, i.e. racial, group called *the* working class. The truth is that 100 per cent of intelligence anywhere comes from the human race. The "accident of birth" accurately expresses the modification that class can make to any given intelligence, but it is an accident, not a predestination. The trend towards racism in Russia is, however, more alarming than this quotation would suggest. Beginning in 1939, the census took into account the race to which each citizen belongs, as well as his native language. The 1937 census, which mentioned "national culture" and not "race," gave "unsatisfactory results" on religion and was never published.

9. A well-known example of the multiform vice of materialism in art shows at once its typical and its ludicrous features. Leonardo's "Mona Lisa," as everyone knows, seems to wear an enigmatic smile, and apparently ever since the portrait was painted nervous people have been asking themselves, "What is she smiling at?" From Vasari to Walter Pater, almost every critic has given his answer. There is the harmless kind that says the smile is "embodied mystery" and there is the materialistic-causal kind, like Taine's, which asserts that the sitter was flirting with the artist. The search for a cause reached its high point in the discovery by Salomon Reinach that Mona Lisa had lost her little daughter shortly before the portrait was painted. So "now we know." She is "smiling as much as she can in the face of sorrow." The only trouble is that in certain lights it is doubtful whether she is smiling at all, just as in the minds of certain scholars (like Dr. R. S. Stites of Antioch College) it is doubtful whether she is Mona Lisa, the bereaved

mother, or Isabella d'Este, whose smile (if any) would require a new search for a fresh cause.

CHAPTER 8

1. The most trustworthy guides are the writings of William James and Henri Poincaré; J. B. Stallo's classic *Concepts and Theories of Modern Physics,* 1882; Norman Campbell's *Physics: the Elements,* 1920, and A. N. Whitehead's great summary, *Science and the Modern World,* 1924. The artistic character of scientific procedure is made explicit in two quotations by practising scientists. Says Mr. J. W. N. Sullivan:—

There are always several laws which will satisfy the observations; the one that is chosen is chosen for its simplicity, i.e. because of the mental satisfaction it affords. [*Aspects of Science,* Jonathan Cape, p. 40.]

And Mr. Norman Campbell, the Cambridge physicist already cited:—

We examine our past experience, and order it in a way that appears to us most simple and satisfactory; we arrange it in a manner that is dictated by nothing but our desire that the world may be intelligible. And yet we find that, in general, we do not have to alter the arrangement when new experience has to be included. We arrange matters to our liking and nature is so kind as to . . . conform to it. If anyone asks, Why? What kind of answer can we possibly give? . . . It must always be remembered that science does not attempt to order all our experience; some part of it, and the part perhaps that is of most importance to us as active and moral human beings, is omitted altogether from the order. And it is very hard to say whether we omit it because we know we cannot order it in the same manner . . . or because we feel that even if we could force it into such an order, that order would not be appropriate to it. The other consideration arises when it is asked who are the "we" to whose intellectual desires nature conforms. . . . The great man of science, like the great poet or the great artist, is born and not made; like the artist he must train his faculties, but training alone will not confer them. . . . It is only the great leaders of science who see the right order.

Notes and Acknowledgments

They and they only can establish an order which satisfies their intellectual desires and yet find that it is valid for the future as well as for the past. . . . The world as we know it is the product of its geniuses . . . and to deny that fact is to stultify all history. [*What Is Science?* Methuen, 1921, pp. 71–73.]

2. Professor Carlton J. H. Hayes's essay "History and the Present" (*Social Studies,* Feb. 1936) admirably states the problem and summarizes the tenable conclusions:—

I defy anyone to treat at any length of any subject (except, possibly, mathematical subjects) without employing to some extent the historical method. We may isolate and assemble some economic data and call the result economics. We may isolate and assemble some political data and label the result political science. But in neither of these instances will the data have much significance unless they are compared and contrasted with similar data from the past and with data from other fields. . . .

And on the vices into which social science has fallen:—

We go ahead, with conviction and enthusiasm, seeking pure facts in the present and quarantining them against infection from the past. It is really far easier to be a social scientist (in this sense) than to be an historian. It is far easier to find facts than to relate or explain them. . . . Man cannot live as the time-animal and the art-animal which he is, without history. He never has, and I am convinced he never will. There may be very faulty history, of course, as written and as taught. There has always been conflict between man's time-sense and his art-sense. . . . There is and can be no absolute objectivity, no pure science, in the writing and teaching of history. . . . Nevertheless we must not be deterred from approaching the ideal of history. And I am sure the more we strive to know and impart about distant ages, as well as about our own . . . the more we shall find history truly enlightening and its method truly serviceable in guarding us against gullibility. . . . [Pp. 76–78.]

3. The attitude of immeasurable superiority supposedly conferred by manual training in the physical sciences is exemplified by H. G. Wells in his *Autobiography* whenever he refers to Shaw and others who, he contends, are only half-educated because they cannot adjust the set-screws of a microscope. He argues that they are dis-

qualified by this ignorance from taking part in the task of social criticism and social betterment. Wells's own effectiveness has been so largely utopian and fictional that one would search in vain for the peculiar precision that scientific training has given his diagnoses and predictions.

4. See R. L. Schuyler, "Indeterminism in Physics and History," *Social Studies,* Dec. 1936, and C. W. Cole, "The Relativity of History," *Political Science Quarterly,* June 1933.

5. In *The American Scholar,* Jan. 1933, p. 36. See also President Angell, "The Scholar and the Specialist," *ibid.,* summer 1937; Dr. Alexis Carrel's Dartmouth Phi Beta Kappa Address, Oct. 11, 1937, and the literature on the "Ph.D. Octopus" from William James to President Lowell (*At War with Academic Traditions in America,* 1934, pp. 207–209). Something of the effect of graduate scholarship on talented young men can be seen in the following excerpt from the letter of a student to his former teacher:—

Z—— University has made me have serious doubts about my decision to take up teaching rather than law. Teaching here is too much cluttered up with meaningless "scholarship." Often literature itself is entirely forgotten. I have even been told that a Ph.D. candidate should not interest himself in modern literature, since that is the function of the critic, and the Ph.D. is not to be a critic! And this from X, who can be very sensible.

6. In James's *Some Problems of Philosophy* (Longmans, Green), pp. 6–7.

7. ". . . In some measure, at least . . ." said W. A. Dunning, "the course of human history is determined no more by what is true than by what men believe to be true; and therefore . . . he who brings to light a past occurrence of which he is the first to have knowledge is likely to be dealing with what is no real part of history." (*Truth in History,* Columbia University Press, 1937, p. 7.)

8. Quoted from Norman Campbell by Sullivan, *op. cit.,* p. 30. The latter also gives an interesting view of James Clerk Maxwell's concerning determinism in science:—

If, therefore, those cultivators of physical science . . . are led to the study of the singularities and instabilities, rather than the continuities of things, the promotion of natural knowledge may tend to remove that prejudice in favour of determinism which seems to

Notes and Acknowledgments

arise from assuming that the physical science of the future is a mere magnified image of that of the past. [P. 56.]

(See also *The Scientist in Action* by W. H. George; "Man Made Truth" in *Mind*, 1938, p. 145; and *The Eighteen Sixties*, ed. by H. Granville-Barker, pp. 255–268.)

CHAPTER 9

1. The interest in words is nothing new. The Socratic method in Plato's *Dialogues* is one long semantic analysis grounded in the same reasons that move Richards, Ogden, and Chase. In the period of the Renaissance, a veritable fever of self-consciousness about words swept Europe, leaving its traces in Rabelais's lists, Montaigne's *Essays,* and Shakespeare's puns. During the French Revolution, pamphlets were written and prizes endowed for the elucidation of key words whose importance to political and social reform was held crucial. The technique had in fact been taught by Bayle and the Encyclopedists, whose influence often resulted from the re-defining of important words.

Early in the nineteenth century, George Campbell wrote an interesting book called *The Philosophy of Rhetoric* (1823), including a very "modern" chapter entitled, "What is the Cause that Nonsense so often escapes being detected both by the reader and by the writer?" Froude, writing about Oxford in 1850, says that at one time there were "so many attachments to words in place of things that the collegian in afterlife became liable to reproach upon his head." Since Froude, the work of Trench, Weekley, Mencken, and Empson forms a continuous line to the present. The whole difficulty is tersely put by Montaigne: "The question is of words, and with words it is answered."

2. Attacking the same absolute, Mr. William Troy admirably states the nature and function of words:—

I believe that a natural history of words might be written; but it would involve nothing less than an account of the whole culture in which they are found . . . individual words taken in and by themselves have only a relative significance, if any significance at all. It is only when they exist in some context, when we can perceive their interrelationships with each other that any single

204

word takes on definition. . . . [*Bennington Report on Science and Culture,* p. 84.]

3. Dr. Armitage Whitman's article in the *New Yorker* for Oct. 9, 1937.

4. The examples given in this section are all genuine. The point of withholding reference to their source is to stress the impersonal prevalence of the failing instead of singling out the authors of the particular offenses.

5. In one of Franco's most coherent speeches, after some fairly "learned" cultural history we get:—

It is necessary to substitute the old conception of the word "obligation" indifferently employed in the democratic liberal constitutions, for the more exact and rigorous one of "duty," which is service, abnegation, and heroism, not imposed by the coercive sway of the law, but respected with the free and voluntary adhesion of the conscience, when our feelings are impregnated with the present spiritual essences. [Speech of April 19, 1938.]

Compare this bit of lexicography with Mussolini's "We have detached ourselves from the too-limited notion of philanthropy, to reach the vaster and deeper notion of assistance. We must make still another step forward: from assistance we must arrive to the full realization of national solidarity." (*Charte du Travail 10° Anniversaire,* p. 269.)

6. The latest example of the use of learned nonsense for political ends occurs in the Prize Essay subject proposed by the Munich Academy in December 1938: "The Swastika being a primitive Aryan symbol [which, by the way, is not true in an exclusive sense], research must be directed to finding the common intellectual origins of India and National Socialism." This "cultural" subject was significantly proposed at a time when Germany had reasons for wishing to annoy India's keeper, Great Britain.

CHAPTER 10

1. The Carnegie Foundation *Reports* are well known. A more recent and particular onslaught is that of Dr. Foster Kennedy of Cornell University Medical School, who, addressing the New York Academy of Medicine on February 7, 1939, proposed the abolition

of the A.B. requirement for the study of medicine. He finds school and college education degraded, useless, and mechanical, the outcome being to turn the profession of medicine into a "union of gadgeteers." (N. Y. *Times,* Feb. 8, 1939.)

2. This debate, called by the *New York World-Telegram* the "great nutbread war," can be followed in that newspaper, March 10, May 6 and 7, 1937, and in the *New York Times* for March 11, 1937, and March 8, 1938.

3. Book I, Ch. 20.

4. Given in a supplement to the bulletin dated July 1937 and written by President Barr and Dean Scott Buchanan.

5. See J. Barzun and R. Valeur, in *Re-Directing Education,* ed. Tugwell and Keyserling, 1935, II, p. 83.

6. On Bard College, see Donald G. Tewkesbury, N. Y. *Times,* Aug. 5, 1934; on Black Mountain College, Louis Adamic, *Harpers,* April 1936 (and criticism by De Voto, same issue); on Bennington College, Robert D. Leigh, "A Progress Report," Feb. 25, 1938; on Sarah Lawrence College, Constance Warren, *Atlantic Monthly,* June 1938, and William Schuman, "Unconventional Case History," *Modern Music,* May 1938.

7. The soundest as well as the most concise thing that has been said on the subject is the statement made by President Lowell of Harvard at the outbreak of World War I. It is reprinted in *At War with Academic Traditions in America,* 1934, pp. 267–272.

8. Said Montaigne: "And those but mock themselves, who think to diminish our debates and stay them by calling us to the express word of sacred Bible." ("Of Experience," *Essays,* Book III, Ch. XIII.)

9. See his *Higher Learning in America,* p. 96.

10. One great difference between the Neo-Aristotelians in our modern universities and Aristotle himself is that they are completely clear, systematic, and have an answer for nearly everything, whereas the philosopher himself, as he stands revealed in his works, is a much more groping, tentative, and many-sided mind.

11. For Music 101, 102, 103, Part II, April 1936, pp. 1–2.

12. James repeatedly warned against the passion for efficiency and "results" in the life of the mind—a passion which leads nowadays to the endless "testing" and "evaluating" of the intangible and imponderable. Writing to his brother Robert in 1868, he says:—

Notes and Acknowledgments

We Americans are too greedy for results . . . and we think only of means of cutting short the work to reach them sooner. . . . I am sure it is a destructive temper of mind in purely intellectual pursuits. . . . [Quoted in R. B. Perry, *Thought and Character of William James,* Atlantic-Little, Brown, Vol. I, p. 258.]

Again, in a letter to Tom Ward of the same year he says:—

Results should not be too voluntarily aimed at or too busily thought of. They are *sure* to float up of their own accord, from a long enough daily work at a given matter; and I think the work as a mere occupation ought to be the primary interest with us. At least, I'm sure this is so in the intellectual realm. . . . [*Letters of William James,* Vol. I, p. 133.]

CHAPTER 11

1. The views in this chapter are naturally based on a reading of history at large and of the classics of political theory from Plato to Marx. I must mention particularly Thucydides, the *Annals* of Tacitus, the *Florentine History* of Machiavelli, and the *Political Essays* of David Hume. (See also two essays by W. L. Westermann, "The Economic Basis of the Decline of Ancient Culture" and "The Ptolemies and the Welfare of Their Subjects," *Amer. Hist. Review,* July 1915 and Jan. 1938.)

2. See Hilaire Belloc and Cecil Chesterton, *The Party System,* London, 1911, particularly "A Note on Collusion," pp. 212–217. Chesterton's brother summarizes the book as follows:—

When the public theory of a thing is different from the practical reality of that thing, there is always a convention of silence that cannot be broken; there are things that must not be said in public. The fact concealed in this case exactly illustrated the thesis of the book called *The Party System;* that there were not two real parties ruling alternately, but one real group, "the Front Benches," ruling all the time. [*Autobiography,* Sheed and Ward, p. 210.]

3. "Names and forms of things seem to change more than things themselves," says C. J. H. Hayes, speaking of the French Revolution. (*Social Studies,* Feb. 1936, p. 79.)

4. See the "Dialogue on Government in the handwriting of Voltaire," printed by Lytton Strachey in *Books and Characters,* p. 142.

5. "The third and last and most important condition [of carrying out the Fascist Revolution] is to live in an atmosphere of high ideal tension." (Mussolini, *The Corporate State*, p. 25.)

CHAPTER 12

1. When James called pragmatism "a new name for some old ways of thinking," he was being, as usual, both modest and accurate. There have always been people who saw, like Montaigne, "how much more ample and diverse the World is, than either we or our forefathers could ever enter into," or who resented, like Blake, the "confident insolence sprouting from systematic reasoning," or who exclaimed, like Matthew Arnold, in the face of rigid systems: "What hideosities, what solecisms, what lies, what distortions, what grimaces, what affectations. . . !"

This perception has always led those who feel it passionately to quarrel with materialism, absolutism, and determinism in culture. In this book it has led me to assume that Mind exists, that experience is trustworthy, and that free will is real. Most readers will be content to leave it at that, but I promised the technical-minded an amplification of the underlying reasons. The chain that links them together is this: if pragmatism describes what man's mind does in science and art (pp. 27–29 of this book) it is clear that it does not *copy* nature but "works" with it (pp. 92–93). The verification of this "work" by "success" makes perception real and experience trustworthy (Norman Campbell quoted, p. 201). It likewise disposes of subjectivism, the doctrine that each man is in a separate universe. Since in discovering reality Mind is active and not passive, the hypothetical Matter of the materialists is needless, for what they talk about is not the perfectly real table or stone we all deal with, but a *substance* which, by their definition, is unknowable and yet the agent of our sensations and ideas. For the pragmatist, things are real, solid, as we know them, and insofar as we know them. But we may and do see them in different ways (pp. 76, 83–84) and must therefore rule out the One, the Absolute, and the predetermined. As for mind, it is in Berkeley's words— which Samuel Butler or Bernard Shaw would endorse—"permanent being, not dependent on corporeal things; nor resulting, nor connected, nor contained, but containing, connecting, enlivening

208

the whole frame; and imparting those motions, forms, qualities, and that order and symmetry, to all those transient phenomena, which we term the Course of Nature." (*Siris*, Fraser ed., III, 264–265.)

2. From *Memories and Studies* (Longmans, Green), pp. 322 and 313.

3. James says so himself in a jotting published by Perry, *op. cit.*, II, p. 383:—

It means anarchy in the good sense. It means *individualism, personalism:* that the prototype of reality is the *here and now;* that there is a genuine novelty; that order is being *won*—incidentally reaped. . . . It means tolerance and respect; it means democracy as against systems which crush the individual. . . . It means hero-worship and leadership. It means the vital and the growing as against the fossilized and the fixed, in science, art, religion, custom, government. It means faith and help; in morals, obligation respondent to demand.

4. The key to the toleration issue lies in the distinction between private and militant absolutisms. Take Cardinal Newman at one end of the scale and Thomas Hardy at the other, both absolutists. For the one, the absolute is a benevolent intelligence who redeems man from the original sin manifested in the chaotic world (*Apologia*, pp. 267–268). For the other, the Absolute is a heedless, unconscious Will whose performance Hardy gives us in *The Dynasts*. There is no necessary conflict of persons between believers in such absolutes and none between either of them and a pluralist. But if Newman should try to make James go to Mass, or if Hardy should try to forbid the publication of James's *Varieties of Religious Experience*, their absolutes would become dynamic dangers to society without being one whit more satisfactory as explanations of a world which all three agree in seeing in its native diversity.

Index

Index

Molière, 51
Monet, C., 34, 59
More, Sir T., 159
Moussorgsky, M. P., 106
Mozart, W. A., 62, 79
Mussolini, B., 31, 41, 43, 137n.

Napoleon, 32, 62, 118n., 168
Newton, Sir I., 54
Nietzsche, F., 40, 104

Olympic Games, 21
Orwell, G., 132

Paine, T., 48
Paradise Lost, 48, 54, 55
Paris Commune, 79
Paris Exhibition (1937), 40
Parliament (England), 15, 52, 167
Pascal, B., 130n.
Pasternak, B., 46
Pavlov, I., 25
Pericles, 67, 167
Perret, A., 40
Phidias, 89
Picasso, P., 35, 36
Pilgrim's Progress, 48, 54, 55
Plato, 141, 158, 159, 171
Pope, A., 65, 69, 105
Prisoner of Chillon, 7
Prokoviev, S., 46
Proust, M., 34n., 58
Puritan Revolution, 48, 52–53, 56
Purcell, H., 54

Rabelais, F., 105, 142
Race: A Study in Superstition, 26, 97n.
Racine, J., 105
Rainbow, T., 53

Raphael, 101
Ravel, M., 34n., 106
Réaumur, R. A. F., 117n.
Renan, E., 116, 120
Ricardo, D., 118
Richelieu, 32, 68, 165
Rimbaud, 34n.
Rimsky–Korsakov, N., 106
Rivera, D., 39, 45
Robespierre, M., 52, 53, 56
Romains, J., 46, 175
Rome, 30, 68, 167
Roosevelt, F. D., 82, 131
Rossetti, D. G., 106
Rouget de Lisle, C. J., 51
Rousseau, J. J., 43, 150
Rude, F., 52
Russia, 3, 10, 40, 41, 43, 103, 106, 168

St. John's College, 144, 155
St. Simon, Duke of, 166
Samson Agonistes, 54
Sartre, J. P., 46
Schiller, J. C. F. von, 40
Schönberg, A., 36, 37
Schuschnigg, K., 21
Scott, Sir W., 72
Severini, G., 41
Shakespeare, W., 36, 45, 62, 72, 77, 105
Shaw, G. B., 105n., 151
Shelley, P. B., 48, 108
Shostakovitch, D., 46
Smith, Adam, 124
Socrates, 15
Sousa, J. P., 70
Spain, 3, 99, 106
Spencer, H., 118
Spinoza, B., 77, 151

Stalin, J., 11, 41, 51, 92, 169
Stavisky scandal, 166n.
Sullivan, L., 40, 69
Swift, J., 75, 163

Taylor, Jeremy, 54
Terror, the, 3, 49, 51–52
Thirty Years' War, 169
Tocqueville, A. de, 23
Tolstoy, L., 62, 71, 103
Turkey, 167
Tyranny of Words, The, 130

United Kingdom, 22n.
United States, 4–6, 12, 22n., 23 ff., 45, 138, 140–141, 147, 162, 174
See also Constitution; Declaration of Independence

Van Dieren, B., 37
Van Gogh, V., 34n., 35, 74, 82
Varèse, E., 37
Varieties of Religious Experience, 72
Villiers, Sir S., 105n.
Villon, J., 41
Voltaire, 161

Wagner, O., 40
Wagner, R., 32–33
Washington, G., 168
Whitman, W., 69, 82
Wigman, Mary, 38
Wordsworth, W., 47–48
World War I, 35, 37, 139
Wren, Sir C., 54
Wright, F. L., 38
Wycherley, W., 54